Legends,
Lies,
and
Cherished
Myths
of American
History

Legends, Lies, and Cherished Myths
of American History

Richard Shenkman

William Morrow
and Company, Inc.
New York

Library of Congress Cataloging-in-Publication Data

Shenkman, Richard.
    Legends, lies, and cherished myths of American
history.

    Bibliography: p.
    Includes index.
    1. United States—History—Miscellanea.
2. Legends—United States. I. Title.
E178.6.S47   1988   973   88-9293
ISBN 0-688-06580-5

Printed in the United States of America

First Edition

1 2 3 4 5 6 7 8 9 10

BOOK DESIGN BY PANDORA SPELIOS

To M. J. R.

Contents

Contents

9
Contents

Author's Note

Americans, despite everything you hear, know plenty of history. They know that the Pilgrims landed on Plymouth Rock, that Teddy Roosevelt charged up San Juan Hill, that Columbus discovered the world is round, and that Eli Whitney invented the cotton gin.

The punch line, of course, is that Americans know all these things but that none of these things are true.

We usually admit that Americans are somewhat ignorant of history, but we don't realize how ignorant. It is not just that a clear majority does not recall that the first ten amendments to the Constitution are known as the Bill of Rights or that people have a hard time remembering that Lincoln was President in the mid-nineteenth century. It is much worse than that. Not only have they forgotten what they should remember, but they have remembered what they should have forgotten.

Thoreau says somewhere that you remember only what is important. What Americans seem to remember from their history, however, is all that's mythical. With time, facts fade. But myths seem to go on and on, whether it is a tale about the Liberty Bell or the nonsense about Lincoln and Ann Rutledge.

Recently Diane Ravitch asked, in a book which revealed that most teenagers are unaware the Constitution was drafted in the second half of the eighteenth century, "What do our 17-year-olds know?" But what do we adults know?

The answer clearly is: less than we think we do. For as it turns out, even many of the best-known stories from history are false.

Americans are not to blame for knowing so much that is not worth knowing. Even historians have been taken in. Myths are not easy to detect. As E. M. Forster wrote, "Nonsense of this type is more difficult to combat than a solid lie. It hides in rubbish heaps and moves when no one is looking."

Discoverers
and Inventors

Christopher Columbus's achievements were so great that people have been willing to believe almost anything about him, no matter how fantastic.

Nothing is better known, for instance, than the story that Columbus convinced people the world is round, not flat. "Before Columbus proved the world was round," the *Encyclopædia Britannica* reported in an advertisement for the publication in 1961, "people thought the horizon marked its edge." Continued the *Britannica*: "Today we know better."

"Indeed we do," one critic has remarked. The authority of the *Encyclopædia Britannica* notwithstanding, it was Aristotle who proved the world is round, pointing out during an eclipse that the earth casts a spherical shadow on the moon. Plato popularized the concept. By Columbus's day it was taken for granted. The story giving Columbus credit for the discovery did not even surface until after he had died.

The person mainly responsible for the myth was Washington Irving. An obscure writer had mentioned it before, but it was Irving who popularized the story in a dramatic and embellished account. The story appeared not in one of Irving's works of fiction but in what was billed as a biography of Columbus.

In Irving's account, Columbus, in need of funds for his trip to the Indies, goes for help to the sages of the University of Salamanca, whom he tells about his "theory" that the world is round and that the best way to go east is to sail west. The "simple mariner" argues for his theory with "natural eloquence," in a plea, "as it were," for "the cause of the new world." Unfortunately Columbus is turned down, the sages being deaf to this entreaty for the exercise of reason and light. Irving laments the outcome but observes: "What a striking spectacle must the hall of the old convent have presented at this memorable conference!"

As prizewinning historian Samuel Eliot Morison remarks, the story is "pure moonshine." Although Columbus did meet with the professors of Salamanca to try to obtain backing for his trip, the "sphericity of the globe was not in question." According to Morison, "the issue was the width of the ocean." The professors thought Columbus had underestimated the width of the ocean. They were right.[1]

A companion story, just as well known, is that Columbus finally got the money needed for his ocean trip after Queen Isabella had pawned her jewels to finance the venture. Not true. Although the queen offered to sell her jewels if that proved necessary, it did not; the voyage was paid for with government funds.[2]

More controversial is Columbus's reputation as the "first" European discoverer of America. Determining "firsts" is often a matter of serious dispute, but in this instance it is not. While Columbus was the first European whose explorations of America had any consequences, he was definitely not the first to explore the New World. The first was a Norseman of whom practically no one has ever heard: Biarni Heriulfson (sometimes Bjarni Herjulfson), whom Morison has dubbed "Number One, indubitable European discoverer of America."*

Biarni is said to have discovered America by accident. Ac-

---

*The argument that we should speak of the Indians' discovery of America can be made. But that's another matter.

cording to Norse sagas, Biarni sighted what is now known to be North America A.D. 985 (or thereabouts), when he was sailing from Iceland to Greenland and was blown off course. After Biarni, other Norsemen made voyages to America. Most notable was the famous Leif Ericsson (son of Eric the Red), who, some fifteen years after Biarni, is thought to have established a little community called Vinland or Newfoundland. The Vinland settlement is said to have lasted about a dozen years until the Norsemen were finally driven off by hostile Indians.

For many years Columbus's defenders discounted the Norse claims in the belief that they did not hold up under close scrutiny. Archaeologists could not find any evidence that Norsemen lived in North America. And Leif's statement that grapes grew abundantly in Newfoundland (hence the name Vinland) was demonstrably untrue. Grapes don't grow in Newfoundland at all. In the early 1960's, however, the remains of a Norse settlement were discovered in northern Newfoundland at a place called L'Anse aux Meadows. And it turns out Leif had been mistranslated, linguists taking him to mean grapes when he meant berries, which are in abundance, just as he said.[3]

Columbus, of course, is still commonly regarded as the modern discoverer of America, but not by everybody. Some believe John Cabot deserves the title.* Cabot claimed to have landed on Nova Scotia in 1497, a full year before Columbus touched the New World, but he kept such poor records the claim has forever remained in dispute and cannot now be settled. A second voyage to America, in the summer of 1498, is similarly in doubt.[4]

But if Columbus may deserve to be called the first modern discoverer of America, he probably shouldn't be embraced uncritically. For while he was undoubtedly a great man, he wasn't necessarily a good man. Unbeknown to much of the public, he was directly responsible for the deaths of thousands of Arawak Indians on Haiti. One historian even believes Columbus should be thought of not as a hero but as a murderer.

His first encounter with the Arawaks could not have gone

---

* Englishmen have been in the forefront of defending Cabot's claims because he sailed under their flag. But Cabot himself was not English. He was Italian. His real name was Giovanni Caboto.

better. He himself wrote that the natives on the island "are so naive and so free with their possessions that no one who has not witnessed them would believe it. When you ask for something they have, they never say no. To the contrary, they offer to share with anyone."

Columbus, however, did not reciprocate the Indians' kindness. Under pressure to bring back riches to Spain, he required Indians over fourteen years old to make regular contributions of gold. Indians who did not comply, according to historian Howard Zinn, "had their hands cut off and bled to death."

Those Indians who weren't killed were often enslaved and shipped to Spain. On one trip, 500 Arawak men, women, and children were loaded onto ships bound for the Old World; during the voyage 200 died. Far from feeling guilty about the practice of slavery, Columbus boasted about it. "Let us in the name of the Holy Trinity," he wrote, "go on sending all the slaves that can be sold." Within two years of Columbus's arrival, says Zinn, half of the 250,000 Indians on Haiti had died "through murder, mutilation or suicide." Under Columbus's Spanish successors the mistreatment continued. In 1515 there were just 50,000 Indians left. In 1550 only 500 remained. By 1650 there were none.[5]

Yet such is the desire for heroes Columbus will probably always be revered. Morison says he ought to be, for although he had his faults, "they were largely the defects of the qualities that made him great. . . ." Haiti's Arawaks might feel different. But they aren't around to protest.*

The distortions of Columbus's record are matched by Amerigo Vespucci's. In his day he was frequently regarded as the first European to touch the American mainland. Later he was recognized as the first person to realize America was not part of Asia but a new continent. In our day he has been credited with inventing a new lunar astronomy.

Not one of these claims is accurate. Vespucci lied about beat-

---

*Howard Zinn chides Morison for acknowledging mass murder on one page, then ignoring it later on. To bury the facts, he says, "in a mass of information is to say to the reader with a certain infectious calm: yes, mass murder took place, but it's not that important—it should weigh very little in our final judgements."

ing Columbus to the mainland in an account of a 1497 voyage that was completely fabricated. Vespucci did not realize he was exploring a new world any more than Columbus did. And he did not invent a new astronomy based on the location of the moon or anything else. Morison, himself an accomplished mariner and a former admiral, says that Vespucci's "claim to have used lunar distances to find longitude is fantastic." The technique had been known in Vespucci's time, writes Morison, "[and] Vespucci is to be praised for having heard about it. But he is merely pulling his reader's leg in implying that he was able to use it. His method, he says, was to turn a primitive plumb-line quadrant or a mariner's astrolabe on its side to measure the angular distance between the moon and a planet, which is impossible, especially at moonrise, with the instruments at his disposal."[6]

America was indeed named after Vespucci, though claims have been made for others. Leif Ericsson has been put forward on the ground that "America" could be construed to mean "Land of Eric." In Scandinavian languages *amt* means "land of." "And so," as one writer puts it, "Amteric ["Land of Eric"] became America." Others have suggested the New World was named after one of John Cabot's friends, Richard Ameryke, the sheriff of Bristol. It is not exactly clear why this should have occurred, but it is supposed to have had something to do with the fact that Cabot had to collect his pension from Ameryke.[7]

Actually America was named after Vespucci by a mapmaker who had been misled by the explorer's apocryphal 1497 adventure. It should not have happened, but it did. And so America, as Ralph Waldo Emerson wrote, must wear the name of the thief "Amerigo Vespucci, the pickle dealer at Seville who . . . managed in this lying world to suppress Columbus and baptize half the world with his own dishonest name."*

*　　*　　*

* Admiral Morison was more indulgent: "So, here's to you, Amerigo. Liar though you were, you made three long transatlantic voyages, wrote entertainingly about them, and played your cards so cleverly as to be elected to the exclusive club of the immortals. Without you, the history of American discovery would be infinitely poorer." (See Samuel Eliot Morison, *The European Discovery of America: The Northern Voyages* [1971], ch. 3.)

Vasco Núñez de Balboa did not lie about his accomplishments, but his reputation as the discoverer of the Pacific Ocean is only partially deserved. The truth is he was not the first European to see the Pacific. He was not even the second or the third to sight it. It is likely that he was the thousandth.

Balboa was first to discover the Pacific from the American side. Of course, there's an Asian side to the ocean. And the Asian side had been explored by Europeans two centuries before Balboa. Marco Polo is said to have sailed on the Pacific on his way to Java in the thirteenth century. In 1375 a European mapmaker featured the western side of the Pacific in a crude drawing of China. Regular European travel on the Asian side of the Pacific began in 1511, two years before Balboa, with the voyages of Antonio de Abreu. Scholars consider Abreu the real discoverer of the Pacific because his voyages to the Spice Islands led to Ferdinand Magellan's exploration of the Pacific.

Balboa's explorations, in contrast, led nowhere. His chief legacy consists almost entirely in the sordid and vicious record he left while blazing his way across Central America to the Pacific. Among other things, he virtually wiped out a village of Indians because the chief liked to dress up in women's clothes. Six hundred people were killed, most by Balboa's man-eating dogs. Balboa himself didn't survive long afterward. After sighting the Pacific, he became entangled in a power struggle with other Europeans for the control of Central America and in 1517 was hanged.[8]

Balboa at least did one thing for which he is famous: sighting the Pacific. Magellan, renowned for circumnavigating the globe, never did make it around the world. Partway through his trip he got in a beach fight with some Filipino natives and was killed. The expedition was finished under the leadership of Juan Sebastián del Cano.

Henry Hudson is rightfully remembered for exploring the Hudson River, but he did not discover the river, the strait, or the bay that bear his name. The river, discovered eighty-five years earlier by Giovanni da Verrazano, did not even seem to interest Hudson. When he realized it was not part of the fabled Northwest Passage, he promptly turned around at Albany and abandoned his exploration.

His chief association with the bay is that he apparently died there under unpleasant circumstances. Autocratic and suspicious, he was left there after his crew revolted against him.[9]

The traditional story told about Sir Walter Raleigh and tobacco is false but not wholly false. Raleigh liked tobacco and was probably responsible for its popularity in England. But he did not introduce it into either England or Europe. Scholars say it was first introduced into England in 1586 by a couple of sea captains. Someone named Thevat reportedly brought it to France in 1556.* There's some evidence other countries may have gotten it even earlier; a couple of sailors supposedly carried some back from Cuba after one of Columbus's expeditions.

As for the most famous anecdote told about Raleigh—that he was once doused with ale by a servant who was alarmed by the tobacco smoke—there's not the least bit of substance to it. Historian Jerome Brooks says the story did not even appear until the eighteenth century, long after Raleigh had died.[10]

Of explorers who came later, two deserve mention, the rivals Robert Peary and Frederick Cook. Both men have been credited with discovering the North Pole, but the truth is neither man may have done so.

Peary's claim that he discovered the Pole on April 6, 1909, is accepted by almost everybody. Almost everybody has included: President Theodore Roosevelt, who upon hearing the news exclaimed, "Bully for Peary!"; the Congress of the United States, which in 1911 commended him for "his Arctic explorations resulting in reaching the North Pole"; and the National Geographic Society, which as recently as 1983 ran a harsh editorial blasting a made-for-TV movie that dared to dispute his claim. Most refer-

---

*Many people have logically assumed that Jean Nicot introduced tobacco into France. Unfortunately, history isn't logical. He didn't.

ence books credit Peary with the discovery; few even hint that the matter's in doubt.

Yet it is in question, as it has been from the very first. Originally doubts surfaced because Peary announced his claim several days after Cook had made *his* announcement. As one writer notes, it seemed odd indeed that a goal which had eluded hundreds of men for centuries had suddenly been achieved by two men almost simultaneously. Later, at congressional hearings, Peary seemed vague about details of the trip, and in several places he contradicted his own writings on the subject, repudiating claims in his own book that several photographs showed him standing at the North Pole (shadows in the pictures proved they couldn't have been taken when he said they had).

More disturbing was the pristine condition of Peary's diary, which suggested to some that he had prepared it after the fact. "It is a well-known fact that on a long Arctic journey," said Congressman Ernest W. Roberts, "ablutions even of the face and hand are too luxurious for the travelers. Pemmican [Indian food made of mixed fat and berries] is the staple article of food. Its great value lies in its greasy quality. How was it possible for Peary to handle this greasy food and without washing his hands write in his diary daily and at the end of two months have that same diary show 'no finger marks or rough usage' . . . ?"

Most disturbing of all was Peary's claim to have traveled an average 26.7 nautical miles a day, a feat, says one historian, "unequaled in the history of polar exploration. By comparison, Cook never claimed to have advanced more than 15 miles a day."

Cook's claim that he discovered the North Pole on April 21, 1908 (which he announced in September 1909, five days ahead of Peary), is unprovable. As he limply explained to critics, he left most of his records in a trunk in Greenland and couldn't substantiate his account. In a later magazine article, he conceded that neither he nor Peary could ever say with certainty that either had reached the Pole because of deficiencies in the measuring instruments.

Belief in the superiority of Peary's claim was based in part on

Legends, Lies, and Cherished Myths

a misleading and vicious campaign directed against Cook. Most serious of all the charges was the allegation that Cook had previously lied about his claim to have scaled Mount McKinley in 1906. The charge was based on the sworn affidavit of his partner on the trip, Edward Barrill, who said he and Cook had fabricated the story. Barrill stuck to his affidavit but later admitted he'd been paid several thousand dollars for drawing it up.

Claims on Peary's behalf were exaggerated by self-interested partisans posing as impartial observers. The most impartial observer of all seemed to be the National Geographic Society, which early on appointed itself arbiter of the Peary-Cook dispute. Unknown to the general public, however, the society had underwritten much of the cost of Peary's trip and had an interest in seeing it succeed. When other institutions around the world seemed poised to award Cook the credit for discovering the North Pole, the society promptly issued a circular imploring them to hold off until after Peary's claims could be examined in detail—by the society. It then awarded Peary the honor after conducting, according to Howard Abramson, merely a cursory examination of the evidence.[11]

Next to the explorers, inventors are a dull lot and have inspired fewer myths. But for fun there's always Eli Whitney, the man who didn't father the system of interchangeable parts.

Misleading accounts of Whitney's contribution to the principle of interchangeable parts, made on the highest authority, have circulated for years. In his day Thomas Jefferson celebrated Whitney as a gunmaker, for inventing "moulds and machines for making all the pieces of his [gun] locks so exactly equal, that . . . the hundred locks may be put together as well by taking the first pieces which come to hand." More recently historian Allan Nevins has credited Whitney with changing the social and economic growth of the United States for his "sustained work in the manufacture of muskets." (In 1798 Whitney was given a lucrative federal contract to supply arms manufactured through the use of interchangeable parts.) The usually reliable *Dictionary of American Biography* as-

Discoverers and Inventors

sures readers that Whitney's system of interchangeable parts succeeded so well that the government was able to save twenty-five thousand dollars annually on arms.

To begin with, Whitney did not devise the principle of interchangeable parts as many people believe. He was not even the first person to try to use it in the manufacture of weapons. More than a decade before he won his contract to make arms for the government, a Frenchman, Honoré Blanc, made firing mechanisms for muskets out of interchangeable parts. Blanc demonstrated his technique at a show attended by Jefferson, who wrote: "He presented me with the parts of fifty locks taken to pieces, and arranged in compartments. I put several together myself, taking pieces at hazzard as they came to hand, and they fitted in a most perfect manner."

To be fair, Whitney himself never claimed to have proposed the principle of interchangeable parts. On the other hand, he did claim to have manufactured firearms for the federal government out of interchangeable parts when in fact, he did not. Peter Baida has reported in the pages of *American Heritage* that "modern researchers have tested the Whitney firearms that survive, with results that astonished those who had grown up believing the Whitney legend. The tests showed that in some respects the parts of Whitney's firearms were not even approximately interchangeable. Moreover, many parts of Whitney's muskets are engraved with special marks—marks that would only be necessary if the manufacturer had failed to achieve interchangeability."

In 1801 Whitney staged a demonstration to prove the interchangeability of his firearms. Historian Merritt Roe Smith says it must have been fixed. "It appears," says Smith, "that Whitney purposely duped government authorities . . . [and] encouraged the notion that he had successfully developed a system for producing uniform parts."[12]

At least there remains the legend that Whitney invented the cotton gin. But if it remains, it does so in the face of the facts.

Daniel Thomas, in an article in 1965 in the *Journal of South-*

ern History, documents that the cotton gin was invented in Asia and perfected in Santo Domingo in the 1740's—half a century before Whitney produced his gin. The Santo Domingo gin was crude but effective. A single slave using the machine could produce up to sixty pounds of fiber a day; a slave working by hand could produce just a pound.

The Santo Domingo gin, however, didn't work on the slippery seeds of American cotton. That was where Whitney came in. His gin was effective on American cotton, but even here his contribution is in question. Whitney's machine was equipped with a wire brush that needed constant cleaning and wasn't very efficient. It was left to one Hodgen Holmes to invent a gin equipped with sawteeth, which allowed for the continuous operation of the device without cleaning. It was Holmes's invention, developed a few years later, which apparently enabled the South to crown cotton as king. [13]

The cotton gin itself is no less wrapped in myth than is Eli Whitney. One often hears, for instance, the belief that the cotton gin triggered the full-scale development of slavery in the South. In fact, while it may have "dug slavery in deeper in the Deep South," as Bernard Weisberger suggests, it may not have had much effect on the rest of the region. Slavery in heavy-tobacco states like Virginia, for example, was at least as strong in the pre-cotton gin period as after. Statistics show that proportionately more Virginia families owned slaves in 1790 (44.9 percent)—before the gin's use—than in 1850, a decade before the Civil War (32.9 percent). Other statistics indicate slavery may have even played a more important role in Virginia in 1790 than later. In 1790 there were sixty-six slaves to every one hundred whites in the state; in the 1850's the figure dropped to fifty-three slaves to every hundred whites. [14]

Like Eli Whitney, Robert Fulton has been given the credit for inventing a thing that he actually helped perfect. The first steamboat was built not by Fulton but by James Rumsey of Virginia in 1784. However, Rumsey's boat, while it worked, did not work well. In an experimental run on the Thames River in London the boat barely hit a high speed of four miles an hour. John Fitch had more success. He built a boat which could carry up to sixty passengers and had a top speed of eight miles an hour. In 1787 Fitch used the boat to take a group of delegates from the Constitutional Convention on a trip up the Delaware River. Still, only Fulton managed to build a steamship powerful enough to be commercially successful in 1807. Well known as it is, Fulton's first steamship is usually misnamed. The old *Encyclopædia Britannica*, like most reference books, called it the *Clermont*. Richard Varick De Witt, the man who painted the most famous picture of the boat, called it the *North River of Clermont*. The official name, recorded in the government's annual "List of Merchant Vessels of the United States," was the *North River Steam Boat*, a name that apparently had been given to the ship because it ran on the part of the Hudson known as the North River. Historian Frank Donovan says Fulton himself called it the *North River Steam Boat* or simply the *North River*. The error of calling it the *Clermont* began after Fulton had died. Scholars have traced the error to Cadwallader Colden, Fulton's first biographer, who may have been confused about the name because for many years the ship docked at a place called Clermont; the biography was published in 1817.[15]

In Thomas Edison's case the confusion has not been over the invention but the inventor himself. Myths to the contrary, Edison did not grow up poor, he did not do badly in school, and he did not forget his wedding day. He did believe in office anarchy, telling a recruit to his laboratory who asked about the rules, "Hell! there ain't no rules around here! We are tryin' to accomplish somep'n." But he denied the story that a train conductor, annoyed by his dangerous experiments, had struck him on the ear and made him deaf.[16]

George Pullman is remembered for inventing the Pullman sleeping car, but sleeping cars were in existence long before his appeared in 1864. The first was built for the Erie Railroad Company by John Stephanson in 1843, and it included fancy diamond-shaped windows. Eli Wheeler patented a sleeping car in 1859.

Legends, Lies, and Cherished Myths

Wheeler lost the patent to Pullman after a long legal battle, but during this court fight evidence of the Erie Railroad car surfaced.[17]

Of all of America's inventors, Henry Ford has historically been the subject of more errors than any other. Among the mistaken impressions: that he single-handedly invented the moving assembly line, that he was something of a progressive for instituting the five-dollar day, and that he was a genius. (Well, he was a genius, but only for a time.)

That Ford is believed to have invented the moving assembly line is an unwarranted deduction from the fact that he installed the first one. Ford himself, however, did not conceive the idea; no individual did. As Ford biographer Robert Lacey points out, it was the joint effort of several of Ford's top engineers.

If the moving assembly line had a single father at all, it was necessity. Sales of the Model T had gone from eighteen thousand cars in 1909–10 to thirty-five thousand in 1910–11 to seventy-eight thousand in 1911–12. People had begun buying the car in such great numbers Ford could not meet the demand for it without dramatically increasing production. Something had to be done, and Ford did it. If he is to be honored, it should be for this: his ability to recognize the necessity for something new and his willingness to try it.

That Ford should be regarded as something of a progressive because of the five-dollar day is the most bizarre of all the myths about him and the most easily refuted. He instituted the five-dollar day mainly to achieve a stable work force and only incidentally to improve the welfare of his employees. As he repeatedly liked to say, the five-dollar day was a matter of "efficiency engineering" with "no charity in any way involved." The assembly line had proved to be a worker's nightmare, and the only way to keep the worker from leaving was to pay him or her better than the usual wage.

Ford undoubtedly felt good about paying a wage that was about double what anybody else in the country was paying. But because of the assembly-line savings, he alone among America's businessmen could afford to pay the higher rate.

He was indeed ahead of his time in employing women, ex-

Discoverers and Inventors

convicts, and the handicapped.* But he hated unions—at a time when unions were in the forefront of the movement for human rights. When labor organizers tried to make inroads at Ford plants, the founder hired a goon squad to beat them up.

Ford undoubtedly was a genius, but sometime around age fifty the magic seemed to disappear. He stuck with the Tin Lizzy long after the public had grown weary of the car, and as a result, he nearly lost everything he'd spent his early years creating. During World War II he took personal charge of the plants working on war-related necessities, but he botched the job so badly some seriously suggested the operation should be nationalized. By the end, as biographer David Halberstam has observed, he who had been known as the creator had come to be regarded as the destroyer. Comments the economist John Kenneth Galbraith: "Against the ineluctable march of bureaucracy . . . Henry Ford had held his own. The company, in consequence, was nearly dead."

He was, of course, one of the great tinkerers of all time, but outside his limited sphere he was uncommonly ungifted. If he could not bolt something or haul it or fix it, he usually had no use for it. History especially seemed beside the point. Put on the stand in a libel trial held to determine whether he was "ignorant," as the *Chicago Tribune* had charged, he forgot there had been a revolution in 1776, acknowledged he didn't have any idea why it had taken place, and said he didn't know who Benedict Arnold was.

One Ford myth is not about the man but about the car. Everyone knows Henry Ford's crack about the Model T: "Any color so long as it's black." What people do not know is that the car did not originally come in black. Until a sharp engineer discovered that black dried faster than any other color, the Model T was painted green with a red stripe.[18]

What Henry Ford was to the automobile, Charles Lindbergh was in some ways to the airplane. But Lindbergh was not, as pop-

---

*In 1919, out of a total work force of about forty-four thousand, Ford employed more than nine thousand handicapped people. Some were missing hands; a few were blind; thirty-seven were said to be deaf and mute.

ularly believed, the first man to fly nonstop across the Atlantic. He was the sixty-seventh person to make the trip. His special accomplishment was that he was the first to fly the route solo.

The first nonstop transatlantic flight was actually made by two British pilots, Sir John Alcock and Sir A. W. Brown, in 1919. But unlike Lindbergh, they did not go from New York to Paris; they flew from Newfoundland to Ireland, a distance of about two thousand miles—fourteen hundred miles shorter than Lindbergh's path. When they reached Ireland, they lost control of their plane and crashed in a bog. A month later a British dirigible carrying thirty-one people made the trip from Scotland to America and then back again, in the first round-trip voyage across the Atlantic. In 1924 a German dirigible with thirty-three on board flew from Germany to New Jersey.[19]

At odds with the American inclination to personalize the inventions of the car and the plane has been the stubborn conviction that some inventions—like the atomic bomb—are such complicated affairs they shouldn't be identified with anyone in particular.

Yet even the atomic bomb was in the end the creation of a very few people, however many thousands worked to produce it. Virtually unrealized by the public, for example, is that a single individual, Leo Szilard, an unemployed Hungarian physicist, has been credited with conceiving the idea of chain reactions. In storybook fashion, he is said to have gotten the idea one day in 1933 in a classic moment of inspiration: standing at a London street corner, waiting for the light to turn green. A year later he patented the idea that the atom could be split, which came to be regarded as one of the key turning points in the development of the bomb.*

Among other people who may be loosely said to have contributed to the development of the atomic bomb is the science fiction writer H. G. Wells. Szilard has explained that he under-

---

* At the time educated opinion had it that atomic energy could never be controlled. In a speech given just several days before Szilard's street corner revelation, Lord Rutherford, a leader in atomic research, noted that talk of using atomic energy was "the merest moonshine." (See Leo Szilard, "Reminiscences," *Perspectives in American History*, Charles Warren Center, Harvard, [1968], Vol. II, p. 100.)

stood the political significance of the idea of the chain reaction because of a book published in 1913 by Wells who describes how two hundred cities are destroyed in a nuclear war started after a scientist discovers—in 1933!—that "atomic disintegration" could release "limitless power."[20]

Founding Fathers

Dozens of attempts have been made over the years to correct the popular impression that the Founding Fathers were above politics. All have failed. The American people insist on believing that the generation that gave us the Declaration of Independence, the Revolution, and the Constitution did not stoop to playing politics, and they will not put up with historians who say otherwise.*It does no good to remind people that Elbridge Gerry, one of the drafters of the Constitution, is held responsible for the political technique of gerrymandering. The generation of the founders has been considered innocent of such a practice and apparently always will be. Nor does it matter if scholars say a thousand times over that Thomas Jefferson fired as many government workers for political reasons as did Andrew Jackson. Jackson popularly remains the great spoilsman. Jefferson stands untainted.[1]

*In Utah Mormon religious leaders teach that the Constitution is a divinely inspired document. Any hint that it was the work of mere men is cause for controversy. If you want a real argument, just go ahead and call the drafters "politicians." But don't expect to make many friends.

In the usual view the founders gave us freedom and equality; scandals like Crédit Mobilier, Teapot Dome, and Watergate came only later. Such is the pristine reputation of the founders that hardly anyone can name even a single scandal with which they were associated. Yet such was the actual state of affairs in the early years that historians tell us that "in all the frauds and tricks that go to make up the worst form of practical politics, the men who founded our state and national governments were always our equals, and often our masters."

Even the debate over the ratification of the Constitution was sullied by political chicanery. In one of the most notorious cases anti-Federalist representatives were dragged from a tavern and forced to attend a meeting of the Pennsylvania legislature so that the Federalists could get a quorum and approve a measure to establish a ratifying convention. To stop the men from leaving the statehouse before the vote was taken, the doors to the building were blocked.

Later the Pennsylvania Federalists bought out a newspaper to prevent it from reporting on their activities. The problem wasn't that the paper, the *Pennsylvania Herald*, was inaccurately reporting the debates on the Constitution. The trouble was that the paper was going about its job all too well, and the Federalists worried that the richly detailed reports on their actions in the ratification debate in Pennsylvania could give their allies trouble in other states. From the time the Federalists bought the paper until the Constitution was ratified, the *Herald* didn't publish one word on the constitutional debate in Pennsylvania, the single most important issue of the day.

More surprising, in light of the absence of controversy in the matter, was the incredible politicking that accompanied the election of George Washington as President in 1789. Everyone knew Washington was going to be elected. But the conflict between the two parties became so ugly in New York that the state legislature—Federalists in the majority in the Senate, anti-Federalists in the Assembly—couldn't decided whom to elect to the electoral college. In the end Washington was elected without any votes from New York. Both houses remained so locked in political combat that they couldn't even agree on the election of the state's two U.S. senators. During the entire first session of Congress New York was unrepresented in the Senate.

Gubernatorial elections were similarly colored by politics. Historians report that in 1792 George Clinton stole the election for governor in New York from John Jay. According to John Bach McMaster, a prominent nineteenth-century historian who investigated the election, Jay had the votes and should have won. Instead, Clinton did, after his supporters had managed to throw out the votes of some of the counties favorable to Jay on the basis of "voting irregularities." In one county the "irregularities" consisted solely in the fact that the ballots had been carried to the capital by an unauthorized agent of the sheriff instead of by the sheriff's deputy, who couldn't carry out his duty because he was sick at home.

Lesser contests were also subject to vote fraud. In 1815 Jeffersonian Republicans in New York disqualified the election of Assemblyman Henry Fellows on the dubious ground that forty-nine votes had been marked "Hen. Fellows" instead of "Henry Fellows." The "defeat" gave the Jeffersonians majority control of the legislature and control over patronage. Eventually the Jeffersonians relented and allowed Fellows to be seated—after they had handed out all the plum political jobs in the state.

It may be that some legislatures in the days of the founders were more corrupt than those in the era of Boss Tweed. In 1795 all members of the state legislature in Georgia, save one, accepted bribes in exchange for their votes in a giant land swindle. Some legislators were given slaves. Most were rewarded with parcels of land ranging up to seventy-five thousand acres apiece. Voters turned out the swindlers at the next election and forced the new legislature to abrogate the land deal, which involved the sale of thirty-five million acres of western lands claimed by Georgia. In the nineteenth century the crooks had the last laugh. The U.S. Supreme Court ruled that the grant of land was a binding contract that couldn't be broken regardless of the circumstances under which it had been negotiated. In 1814 Congress awarded more than four million dollars in compensation to people with claims to the land.[2]

Shocking as the extent of political corruption under the founders may be, it can still be explained away as the work of only a relatively few bad apples (except perhaps in Georgia). More troubling may be the well-nigh universal attitude among the founders toward democracy. Historian Charles Beard writes that most of the drafters of the Constitution viewed "democracy as something rather to be dreaded than encouraged." Well into the nineteenth century, he insists, "the word ["democracy"] was repeatedly used by conservatives to smear opponents of all kinds." Even so stout a defender of the people's rights as Jefferson never publicly identified himself as a democrat. Throughout his long life he preferred to call himself a republican, and he used that term even after many of his own supporters had begun to call themselves democrats.[*]

So controversial was the word "democrat" that it does not appear in any of the famous documents associated with the birth of the country—not in the Declaration of Independence, the U.S. Constitution, or any of the state constitutions.

The chief objection to the word was its long association with the Cromwellian revolution in England, where it was used by conservatives to stigmatize political action by the "rabble." Among prominent eighteenth-century Americans, only Anne Hutchinson and Roger Williams, both self-professed radicals, seemed willing to use the word positively. According to Beard, neither James Madison nor Andrew Jackson ever publicly identified himself as a democrat. The party of Jefferson and Jackson did not even come to be known as the "American Democracy" until 1844. Before then the party referred dually to the "Democratic faith" and to their "Republican fellow citizens."

The word "democrat" was held in disrepute for so long that Americans generally only began calling themselves democrats in

---

[*]In his inaugural address in 1801 Jefferson significantly did not say, "We are all Democrats—we are all Federalists." Ignoring the fact that he had run on the Democratic-Republican ticket, he said, "We are all Republicans—we are all Federalists."

Legends, Lies, and Cherished Myths

the twentieth century. Beard writes that the idea that the United States "is first and foremost a democracy" wasn't firmly established until Woodrow Wilson turned the war against Germany into a war for democracy. "In the circumstances," observes Beard, "even Republicans could scarcely repudiate [the term] without acquiring a subversive tinge."[3]

That the founders believed in equality is no more true than they believed in democracy. The Declaration of Independence may say it, but the founders didn't believe all men are created equal. They apparently believed all men are created equal in the eyes of the law, and that was all. They did not believe men are socially or economically equal and didn't believe they should be. As colonial historian Jack Greene puts it, "no idea was farther from their minds. When they talked about equality in a social or economic sense, they meant no more than that each man should have an equal right to achieve the best material life he could within the limits imposed upon him by his ability, means, and circumstances." Put another way, the all-American founders didn't believe in the all-American concept that any all-American boy can grow up to be President.[4]

Misinformed as many people are about the founders, most are aware that the Founding Fathers never wanted the general public to elect Presidents directly. Less well known is that the founders didn't particularly want the electoral college to make the decision either—and didn't think it would. The expectation was that in most cases the electors would deadlock, throwing the contest into the House of Representatives. James Madison predicted that would happen nine times out of ten. George Mason, a delegate to the Constitutional Convention, put the odds at forty-nine out of fifty.[5]

Another myth about the founders is that they have always been revered. In truth, some of those now considered most important have only recently been elevated to the national hall of fame. Sixty years ago Jefferson was still regarded with suspicion or with indifference by many Americans. In the 1920's, when Theodore

Kuper began organizing a national campaign to preserve Monticello, he discovered that he had trouble raising the money needed just to make a hundred-thousand-dollar down payment on the property. "We also found," Kuper reported, "that the textbooks passed over Jefferson by mere mention of his Presidency and his signing the Declaration, and even second-hand book shops were surprised when anybody inquired for a book on Jefferson."

Madison's contributions were popularly recognized even later than Jefferson's. Historian Michael Kammen says Madison's now-famous essay in *The Federalist Papers*, No. 10, did not become famous until the 1950's. He adds that since then, however, it has probably been more "closely scrutinized . . . than either the Declaration of Independence or the Bill of Rights."

Franklin and Hamilton both are said to have come into their own, after years of eclipse, only in the Gilded Age, when Americans became receptive to the avowedly materialistic approaches to life.

Paul Revere rode into the hero's spotlight only in 1863, when Henry Wadsworth Longfellow wrote his famous poem about him, rescuing Revere from virtual obscurity. Historians say before the poem many Americans were not even familiar with Revere's name. In the early nineteenth century not a single editor included Revere in any compendium of American worthies, and Revere did not rate a mention in William Allen's comprehensive biographical dictionary, though there was room enough to list the accomplishments of seven thousand other people. After the poem's publication Revere's stock rose dramatically. Less than ten years later he made his way into Francis Samuel Drake's *Dictionary of American Biography*. Later J. P. Morgan reportedly offered to buy one of Revere's silver punch bowls for a hundred thousand dollars. By the end of the century Revere's reputation had improved so immensely that the Daughters of the American Revolution turned his home in Boston into a museum.

Washington was regarded as an American hero in his own lifetime, of course, but until relatively recently he was also the target of sharp attacks. In his own day he was roughly savaged by editors who frequently treated him with utter contempt. From the Philadelphia *Aurora*, published by Benjamin Franklin's grandson, came this cavil: "If ever a nation was debauched by a man, the American nation has been by Washington." When he died, the paper rejoiced: "Every heart, in unison with the freedom and happiness of the people, ought to beat high in exultation, that the name of Washington ceases from this day to give a currency to political iniquity and to legalize corruption." In the nineteenth century Washington was regarded almost as a saint, but in the 1920's he again came under fierce assault by people who seemed to take satisfaction in tearing him down. Washington, who in earlier accounts seemed incapable of doing anything wrong, now appeared capable of doing nothing right. Something of the flavor of the attacks can be gleaned form a biography by W. E. Woodward, which opens on a characteristically sour note. "Washington," Woodward writes, "came of a family that must be called undistinguished, unless a persistent mediocrity, enduring many generations, is in itself a distinction. With the exception of the illustrious George there is no record of a Washington who ever attained anything more than a quickly fading celebrity."[6]

Especially dear to the right-wing crowd is the belief that the Founding Fathers were devout churchgoers. Compared with modern-day politicians, they perhaps were. But there's not much evidence they were regular worshipers, at least not with regard to many of the most famous founders. Through most of his presidency Washington did not go to church except on special occasions. Neither Jefferson nor Franklin regularly went to church either. John Adams did. Alexander Hamilton during most of his life did not.

Claims that the Founding Fathers were particularly religious are plainly false. While virtually all believed in the divinity of Christ, most remained somewhat skeptical of religion and usually referred ambiguously in correspondence to Providence rather than to Christ Himself or God. Debunker Rupert Hughes reports that in political matters Washington went out of his way to avoid invoking the authority of Christ. When the Continental Congress in 1776 decreed a day of fasting and prayer "to confess and bewail our manifold sins . . . through the merits and mediation of Jesus Christ," Washington omitted the reference to Christ when he repeated the admonition to his troops. In his dying hours Washington, a self-styled deist, never mentioned God or religion, and he left no money for religious causes in his will.

Franklin is said to have believed in the divinity of Christ but is also reported to have thought that there might be other gods as well. He apparently believed strongly in an afterlife; when his brother John died in 1756, Franklin told grieving relatives not to be too anxious since all would eventually be rejoined in some kind of heaven. "Why should you and I be grieved at this," he wrote, "since we are soon to follow, and know where to find him?"

Jefferson, oddly enough, was probably more religious than Washington, but remained iconoclastic to the end. He was a regular Bible reader, publicly announced that he was a Christian, and even wrote a little book on the "morals of Christ." But he also thought Christ's statements were "defective" because when He was crucified, He hadn't yet reached his peak development as a thinker.

Hamilton poses special problems. He was religious at the beginning of his life and at the end, but not in the middle. In college, according to his roommate, Hamilton was in the habit of "praying upon his knees both night and morning." From 1801, when his political career began to decline, to 1804, when he was killed by Aaron Burr, he again was intensely religious. But in between those periods, Hamilton's religiosity is in doubt. Historian Douglass Adair is of the opinion that during the Revolution Hamilton was utterly indifferent to religion. As secretary of the treasury he began to speak the language of religion and earned a reputation as a Christian statesman, bemoaning the Jacobin, anticlerical, irreligious beliefs of his opponents (especially Jefferson). But Adair concludes that Hamilton's religiosity was "opportunistic," that "forgetting Christ's distinctions between those things which are God's and those which are Caesar's," Hamilton "attempted to enlist God in the Federalist party to buttress that party's temporal power."[7]

Presidents

George Washington is remembered not for what he was but for what he should have been. It doesn't do any good to point out that he was an "inverterate land-grabber," and that as a young man he illegally had a surveyor stake out some prize territory west of the Alleghenies in an area decreed off limits to settlers. Washington is considered a saint, and nothing one says is likely to make him seem anything less. Though he was a wily businessman and accumulated a fortune speculating in frontier lands, he will always be remembered as a farmer—and a "simple farmer" at that.

Even his personal life is misremembered. While Washington admitted despising his mother and in her dying years saw her infrequently, others remembered his mother fondly and considered him a devoted son. While his own records show he was something of a dandy and paid close attention to the latest clothing designs, ordering "fashionable" hose, the "neatest shoes," and coats with "silver trimmings," practically no one thinks he was vain. Though he loved to drink and dance and encouraged others to join him, the first President is believed to have been something of a prude.[1]

The most ridiculous of all the claims is the business about his alleged prudishness. In his youth he so openly showered his affections on Sally Fairfax, the wife of his best friend, that he was suspected of having an affair with her. As a soldier he displayed the usual soldierly interest in crude sexual jokes. Once, when writing about a failed love affair involving his former aide, Colonel Joseph Ward, Washington remarked that Ward, "like a prudent general," should have "reviewed his *strength*, his arms, and ammunition before he got involved in an action." In the future, Washington advised, Ward should "make the *first* onset upon his fair del Toboso, with vigor, that the impression may be deep, if it cannot be lasting." On another occasion Washington joked about a jenny that, "like a true female," seemed to enjoy being penetrated by a disproportionately sized jackass.[2]

Debunkers have sometimes tried to prove that Washington was an out-and-out womanizer, but there doesn't seem to be any evidence he was. The charge that he slept with Sally Fairfax, for instance, is rejected by his most responsible biographers, including James Thomas Flexner, who probably would have been delighted to discover otherwise. Washington loved Fairfax, and the year before he died, he wrote her a letter in which he said she had provided him with the happiest moments of his life. But neither he nor she ever hinted at a physical relationship, and no one else has ever been able to produce any proof that one existed.

The myth that Washington fathered several children by his slaves is completely at odds with the known record. Washington treated his slaves with respect and compassion and never once is known to have made any advances toward them. The only such "evidence" is found in a letter circulated by the British during the Revolution. In the letter Washington says he had an assignation with "pretty little Kate, the Washer-Woman's daughter." Washington, however, never wrote the letter; it was a fraud, the product of British propaganda.

The erroneous charge that Washington died from a bout of pneumonia after a secret winter rendezvous with a black concubine has survived because it contains a tiny seed of truth. He did die after coming down with a winter cold, but it wasn't he who was out romping with the slaves. It was his plantation manager, Lund Washington, who is known to have fathered a child by a black mistress.

George, by the way, probably couldn't have fathered a child by anybody. While Washington always said he wanted children, he and Martha never had any, the difficulty almost certainly being with George, not with Martha. As Flexner points out, in her previous marriage, Martha had four children in seven years, the last child just two years before her marriage to Washington. In view of Martha's proved fecundity, it appears logical to conclude that George was sterile.[3]

Somewhat at odds with the debunker's picture of Washington as a swinger is his legendary reputation as something of a cold fish. When Gouverneur Morris, it is said, slapped the President on the back in a gesture of good fellowship, Washington is supposed to have "fixed his eye upon Morris for several minutes with an angry frown, until the latter retreated abashed." The fact is that Washington was somewhat unapproachable and contrived to keep his distance from people, especially after he became President. But while he may have appeared aloof, he was hardly unemotional. That he seems so is testament to his iron ability to keep his passions in check. Friends reported that Washington was actually a volcano of powerful emotions and often seemed on the verge of exploding in tremendous anger. During the dark days at Valley Forge, when the Congress refused to send supplies needed to feed his starving troops, he frequently did explode. In letter after letter Washington raged at Congress, at times suggesting the government wasn't worthy of the patriotic efforts being waged on its behalf. Occasionally, when soldiers got to fighting with one another, he so lost his temper that he personally intervened to stop them. One time he started knocking heads around when some feisty drunken soldiers began arguing.[4]

I come now to the matter of Washington's false teeth, which have attracted considerable attention. He did wear false teeth, but alas for the humorists, there wasn't anything funny about them. For one thing, they fit badly. At the height of the Revolution Washington was occasionally preoccupied not with the state of the war but with the state of his teeth. When he heard that a French dentist of considerable skill had come through the lines from New York, Washington hurriedly inquired if the man was really as accomplished as rumor had it. Assured he was, Washington invited the Frenchman to his army headquarters. The visit was arranged even though it entailed the risk that the British might find out about it and, as they had in the past, poke fun at Washington for his dental difficulties. Unfortunately the French dentist proved no more able than others to cure Washington of his pains, which continued to such an extent that he often ended by having his teeth pulled. By the time he died his false teeth were anchored to a single tooth, the only tooth left in his mouth.[5]

Finally, there is the matter of the cherry tree story, which is so well discredited it hardly needs refuting. But to set the record straight, in the original story told by Parson Weems, Washington doesn't chop down the cherry tree; he barks it.[6]

Like Washington, Thomas Jefferson has been the target of innumerable sexual innuendos. But the chief charge—that he carried on for years with a beautiful slave named Sally Hemmings—seems to have had more substance that the criticisms leveled against Washington.* Whether it's true, however, is a matter of opinion. Biographer Fawn Brodie says it is; Dumas Malone, one of the foremost authorities on Jefferson in the world, wrote that it couldn't be because Jefferson wouldn't have permitted himself to do something so tawdry as to have sex with a woman who wasn't in a position to say no.

* Here, in brief, is what is known: Jefferson was home about the time each of Hemmings's children was conceived; one child is said to have closely resembled him; as they grew up, he reportedly gave the children special treatment; when they turned twenty-one, he gave them their freedom, and the only slaves he ever freed were Hemmingses. Whether he was attracted to Sally no one knows. But everyone said she was beautiful, and she may have reminded him of his dead wife since they were almost certainly half sisters. Their father was John Wayles, Sally's original master. (See Dumas Malone, *Jefferson the President: First Term* [1970], pp. 494–98, appendix 2; and Winthrop D. Jordan, *White over Black* [1969], pp. 461–69.)

No less confusing than his relationship with Sally Hemmings was Jefferson's position on the press. Evidence abounds that he was both its champion and its scourge.

All important is the question of which Jefferson one is talking about, the Jefferson of words or deeds. No writer was ever more eloquent in defending the press than Jefferson. It was he who remarked in 1787 that "were it left to me to decide whether we should have a government without newspapers, or newspapers without a government, I should not hesitate a moment to prefer the latter." But as a politician Jefferson frequently lashed out at the press and used the government to try to put hostile publishers out of business. After he became President, he became so fed up with Federalist criticism of his administration that he encouraged the states to prosecute "tory" newspapers for seditious libel. In 1806 he stood by silently when one of his own judicial appointees won federal grand jury indictments for seditious libel against several Federalists, including a clergyman. Jefferson eventually spoke out against the indictments—after he had learned the trials would focus on an affair he had with a married woman in 1768.*

Jefferson, of course, helped establish some of America's most basic freedoms, but freedom of the press was not one of them. And compared with the ideas of many of his contemporaries on freedom of the press, his were not enlightened. When the Bill of Rights was under discussion, James Madison supported complete freedom of the press; Jefferson, however, said he believed the press had only the right to print the truth. Jefferson seemed blind to the fact, as one historian put it, that "in politics one's man's truth is another's falsity."[7]

One other myth involving Jefferson deserves mention. Because Presidents nowadays address Congress in person, it's believed they always have. Yet between John Adam's administration and Woodrow Wilson's, not one chief executive personally addressed Congress. Jefferson is responsible for the lapse. When he became

*This is one affair about which there's no doubt. While he was President, Jefferson acknowledged that as a young bachelor he had "offered love to a handsome lady," the wife of a neighbor, Mrs. John Walker. (See Dumas Malone, *Jefferson the Virginian* [1948], pp. 153–54, appendix 3.)

President, he instituted the practice of sending Congress only written messages. A poor speaker, he didn't want to put himself in the awkward position of doing something he didn't do well.[8]

Myths about James Monroe are few, but one seems to have become entrenched and is worth refuting: the belief that in 1820 a tradition-conscious member of the electoral college, William Plumer, voted against Monroe to deprive the Virginian of the honor of unanimous election. As the story goes, Plumer supposedly wanted to make sure that Washington retained the distinction of being the only President elected without dissent.

Plumer did cast the only negative vote against Monroe, but he did not vote that way out of concern for tradition. According to modern historians, Plumer voted against Monroe for the simple reason that he objected to Monroe's big spending plans.

Nineteenth-century historian James Schouler is held responsible for spreading the myth. Where he got it no one seems to know.

Plumer, incidentally, was pledged to Monroe even though he wound up voting for John Quincy Adams. A lot of people think electors have to vote for the candidates to whom they're pledged, but except in a few states which legally bind electors to their pledges, they don't. In most states, one historian has written, electors are "as free as the air."[9]

Fundamental to many of the myths about Andrew Jackson is the belief that he was a true democrat. Scholars say Jackson was actually something of an aristocrat and point out that he was so regarded by his friends in Tennessee, where he owned a good part of present-day Memphis and was treated with deference by the local citizenry. He may have grown up on the frontier and sometimes been crude, but he dressed sharply and had excellent manners—so excellent that Frances Trollope, a foreign visitor noted for her dyspeptic view of Americans, said that Jackson, unlike most of his countrymen, was a gentleman. It's true that when he has inaugurated, he invited commoners to the White House to celebrate. But he did not regularly seek their company; most of his close friends were wealthy.[10]

Much of the confusion stems from the loose way in which the word "democrat" is thrown around. The fact that Jackson was a bad speller, for instance, is used to prove he was "just like us," though bad spelling proves only that he was a bad speller. More to the point may have been the stories about his contempt for good spellers. According to one story, Jackson is supposed to have told a friend he never thought much of a man who could think of only one way to spell a word. But who knows if he ever really said such a thing?

The myth that Jackson made a fool of himself at Harvard when he was given an honorary degree in 1833 has reinforced the idea that he was just plebeian. In the story, Jackson is so impressed by a speech given in Latin by a Harvard luminary that he clumsily attempts a little Latin when it is his turn to speak. Standing before the crowd of scholars, Jackson is supposed to have strung together what presumably were the only two Latin phrases he allegedly knew and to have said: "*E pluribus unum*, my friends, *sine qua non.*"

In fact, Jackson never said any such thing at Harvard. But it wouldn't have been considered improper by many people even if he had. While the Whigs used the story to try to discredit Jackson—it was a Whig who invented it—Jackson supporters said it demonstrated their man's superb ability to best the overeducated at their own rhetorical games. Shrewdly turning the tale to their advantage, Jacksonians claimed that "*E pluribus unum, sine qua non*" was merely a brilliant way of summing up the nationalistic sentiment "Our Federal Union, it must be preserved." Jackson's aide Josiah Quincy remarked that the Harvard story was, "on the whole, so good, as showing how the man of the people could triumph over the crafts and subtleties of classical pundits, that all Philistia wanted to believe it." Biographer John William Ward remarks, "Precisely."[11]

Of all the myths about Jackson, none is more widely believed than that he was violently short-tempered, so violent that one contemporary wrote that the President was "but little advanced in civilization over the Indians with whom he made war." Jackson acknowledged he was often represented "as of a savage disposition" and as a man who "allways [sic] carried a scalping knife in one hand, and a tomahawk in the other, allways ready to knock down, and scalp any and every person who differed with me in opinion."

Jackson did have a bad temper, especially when he was young. But as he grew older, according to contemporaries, he became far less volatile. As President he seemed in such remarkable control of his feelings that Martin Van Buren observed that "in times of peculiar difficulty and danger" Jackson remained calm "and always master of his passions." One historian has remarked that if Jackson was as out of control as people seem to think, he surely would have become violent when false attacks were made on his wife's virtue. "That he did restrain himself," Albert Somit points out in a study published in a southern historical periodical, "is a monumental tribute to his powers of self-control, so belittled by those whose lives would otherwise have been greatly endangered."[12]

Abraham Lincoln has inspired so many myths that Americans may be surprised to learn some of the most delightful stories about the sixteenth President are essentially true.

As a defense lawyer Lincoln used a common almanac to show that his client had been framed for a murder. In a dramatic scene, replayed in a popular movie about the President, Lincoln proved that a key prosecution witness, who claimed to have seen the murder by the light of a full moon, couldn't have. The almanac showed the moon wasn't full that night.

Strongly superstitious, Lincoln once peered into an old mirror and, seeing two images of himself, took the incident to mean he would be elected to a second term but would not live to complete it.

He did indeed keep important letters and documents inside his hat.

And he grew his beard at the suggestion of an eleven-year-old girl.[13]

What's more, he was tall. He really liked to crack jokes. He had been a rail splitter. He didn't like slavery.

He didn't like to be called Abe, and nobody called him Abe. According to biographer Stephen Oates, "he loathed the nickname." His wife, Mary, called him Mr. Lincoln or Father. Friends called him Mr. Lincoln or simply Lincoln. When writing to friends, Lincoln routinely signed off "A. Lincoln."[14]

The famous failed love affair he is said to have had with Ann Rutledge—the "only woman" Lincoln ever loved—never happened. And he never said afterward, "My heart lies buried there." Oates says: "There is no evidence whatever that Lincoln and she ever had a romantic attachment. There is no evidence that theirs was anything more than a platonic relationship." He *did* have a relationship with one Mary Owens and in 1836 indicated he wanted to marry her. But in 1837 he backed out, saying he wasn't sure he could provide for her properly.[15]

Lincoln's train trip to Washington for his first inaugural is shrouded in myth. At the time journalists reported that because of assassination rumors, he sneaked into the capital wearing a Scottish plaid cap and a long military coat. One cartoonist featured Lincoln doing a dance dressed in Scottish kilts; the cartoon was headlined "The Mac Lincoln Harrisburg Highland Fling." In the 1940's the Chicago *Sun* and the Chicago *Tribune* said that Lincoln had ridden into Washington hidden by "eye-shields" and armed with "iron fighting knuckles."

In actuality, Lincoln was smuggled into Washington aboard a special sleeping car which had been deceptively reserved in the name of his guard's invalid brother. The story about the Scottish cap was mischievously invented by a New York reporter, Joseph Howard.[16]

That Lincoln hurriedly composed the Gettysburg Address on the back of an envelope while on his way to deliver the speech is not true. Nice as it might be for this most impressive of speeches to have been dashed off in a moment of inspiration, it seems rather to have been the result of more mundane efforts of writing and rewriting. Several drafts of the speech have been discovered; one draft is written in Lincoln's own hand on executive stationary.[17]

Though Lincoln was a great orator, he gave far fewer speeches as President than is popularly believed. While his critics frequently and loudly bemoaned his handling of the war, he reacted usually by silence. As he explained to a Maryland crowd in 1862, "In my present position, it is hardly proper for me to make speeches." He seemed particularly afraid of saying something offensive in an off-the-cuff remark. When a crowd gathered to greet him at the Gettysburg train station, he refused to say anything lest he say something "foolish."[18]

In the years immediately after he was killed, Lincoln became enmeshed in dozens of religious myths. In the most famous one preachers ascribed significance to the fact that Lincoln died on Good Friday. A Connecticut clergyman declared that it was not "blasphemy against the Son of God" to announce "the fitness of the slaying of the Second Father of our Republic on the anniversary of the day on which He was slain. Jesus Christ died for the world, Abraham Lincoln died for his country."

Lincoln stories have become less apocalyptic. No one now would probably go so far as to describe Lincoln as a kind of George Washington-Moses-Christ figure all rolled into one the way people used to do. Today the main error is to regard Lincoln as something of a frontier folk hero.

Although he did tell jokes to relieve the burdens of his office, and he was a bit raw around the edges in a frontier kind of way, he was nothing like the sentimental character most people imagine. Friends like William Herndon reported that he was fiercely ambitious, that he appeared homely rather than heroic, and was, unlike the stereotypical westerner, subject to bouts of extreme hopelessness. Though he is remembered vaguely as a "people's lawyer," representing widows and orphans, he also defended corporations, including the Illinois Central Railroad.

Finally, there's the question of his attitude toward blacks. He disliked slavery, but he wasn't an abolitionist. Although he opposed the extension of slavery, he believed that to save the Union, slavery ought to be left untouched where it was, and although he is known as the Great Emancipator, his Emancipation Proclamation didn't end slavery since it applied only to the states that had rebelled, where Lincoln didn't have any authority. Moreover, though he had the support of many radicals, he was critical of radical abolitionists like John Brown and supported Brown's execution. After Elijah Lovejoy, the antislavery editor, had been killed by a proslavery mob, Lincoln made a little joke out of his death in an insensitive speech to a Worcester, Massachusetts, audience: "I have heard you have abolitionists here. We have a few in Illinois and we shot one the other day." [19]

William McKinley is often remembered for saying that God told him to annex the Philippines, a claim that's been used against him to prove his sanctimonious slipperiness. An honest man, it's said, would have admitted that public opinion pushed him to keep the Philippines, that God had nothing to do with the matter.

The story has the advantage of having been originally related by a McKinley sympathizer, General James Rusling. Rusling, a Methodist, said he and some coreligionists heard the statement at a meeting with McKinley in 1899. He later published a long, verbatim account in the *Christian Advocate*. McKinley was quoted as having said he had "walked the floor of the White House night after night until midnight," agonizing over his decision. "I am not ashamed to tell you gentlemen," he reportedly explained, "that I went down on my knees and prayed Almighty God for light and guidance more than one night."

In fairness to McKinley, the story appeared three years after his death and was never corroborated. It's not clear Rusling was even present at the Methodists' meeting. But even if he had been, historians have wondered how he managed to quote McKinley's remarks so extensively without the benefit of a shorthand reporter. Some suggest Rusling just made it all up. Historian Thomas Bailey observes, "Suspicion is thrown on this tale by a book that Rusling had earlier published in 1899, in which he had Lincoln report, in suspiciously similar language, a prayerful experience on the eve of the Battle of Gettysburg." [20]

Theodore Roosevelt, assisted by a host of credulous biographers, is responsible for the myth that as a child he overcame a terrible condition of asthma through a program of vigorous exercise. In reality, according to biographer David McCullough, Roosevelt had stopped suffering from asthma long before he took up the physical activities to which he later attributed his cure. Bodybuilding, pugilism, ranching—all came afterward.

The chief factor in his physical recovery seems to have been his removal from the family setting. When he went to Harvard, says McCullough, his illness magically disappeared.

In fact, Roosevelt may never have had as bad a case of asthma as he claimed. While everyone agrees Roosevelt suffered as a child, McCullough suggests the illness may have been largely psychosomatic. A true victim would presumably have suffered in response to certain physical stimuli. Roosevelt's attacks came during all seasons, morning and night, in the city and in the country. The only thing virtually all the attacks had in common was that they occurred on the same day of the week, Sunday. McCullough says the significance of this is that Sunday was the one day of the week when Roosevelt's father was home and could take care of him. In short the attacks may have been simply an attention-getting device from a son who craved fatherly affection.

Roosevelt was not starved for affection when he was well, but when he was sick, says McCullough, his family indulged him unrelentingly. Because they were rich, their indulgences took on extraordinary dimensions. A single cough could set in motion a whirl of events, from the calling of an impressive horse-drawn carriage to whisk Roosevelt off to the country to the summoning of doctors, maids, and family members. To quote McCullough, "The ocean breezes at Long Branch do not suffice, so off he is taken to Saratoga. Visits to Philadelphia are arranged whenever need be. Or summers in the country. Or a year in Europe." Anything to help little Teedie, as Roosevelt was known, anything at all. (Which makes rather understandable his son's later remark that "When [F]ather goes to a wedding, he wants to be the bride; when he goes to a funeral, he wants to be the corpse.")[21]

Warren Harding, though less important than most Presidents, may have been the victim of more myths than any other. Of these, the things said about his personal behavior were the most damaging. Frederick Lewis Allen wrote that Harding's "private life was one of cheap sex episodes," that he was known for "clandestine meetings in disreputable hotels," that he had sex in the Senate Office Building, and, worse, that he even once got it on in a "coat-closet in the executive offices of the White House itself." Theodore Roosevelt's daughter, Alice Roosevelt Longworth, claimed that Harding was a slob. Journalist William Allen White said he was a "he-harlot." Others said he was a sloth, a drunk, and an incurable cardplayer. Summing up, Alice Longworth said his White House was like a speakeasy: "The air heavy with tobacco smoke, trays with bottles containing every imaginable brand of whiskey stood about, cards and poker chips ready at hand—a general atmosphere of waistcoat unbuttoned, feet on the desk and the spittoon alongside."

Harding was indeed an adulterer. But he seems to have had just two extramarital love affairs, hardly consistent with his reputation as an incessant philanderer. The more notorious affair involved Nan Britton, who claimed in 1927 that Harding had made love to her after he became President and that he had fathered her child. She never filed a paternity case against him, however, and couldn't produce any proof they had had a relationship. She claimed she had burned his love letters, but to this day no one knows whether she was lying or telling the truth.

In the 1960's there surfaced some two hundred love letters that gave indisputable evidence of Harding's relationship with Carrie Phillips, the beautiful wife of a Marion, Ohio, businessman. But the affair, which began in 1909, ended in 1920, before Harding assumed the presidency. At least one Harding apologist, Paul Johnson, hints that the letters don't prove anything more than that Harding, "a pathetically shy man with women," had a "sad and touching friendship" with Phillips. But his interpretation doesn't seem to square with many of the letters' heavy sexual innuendos. "I love you garb'd," Harding wrote at one point, "but naked, *more!*"

There doesn't seem to be the least foundation for any of the other charges, though Harding was guilty of hypocrisy. While he supported Prohibition, he drank in the White House, though always in private quarters and never to excess. He indeed liked to play cards and is said to have indulged in playing poker twice a week. But he wasn't lazy—at least not according to his chief biographer, Robert Murray. Murray says that if anything, Harding was one of the hardest-working Presidents in history. At his desk by 8:00 A.M. almost every day, he usually didn't retire until midnight. "Indeed," says Murray, with some imprecision, "he worked harder as president than either [Woodrow] Wilson or [Theodore] Roosevelt and twice as hard as [William Howard] Taft."

The claim that Harding was chosen as the Republican presidential candidate in a "smoke-filled room" stems from a prediction his campaign manager, Harry Daugherty made before the Republican National Convention. Daugherty asserted that Harding would be selected at "about eleven minutes after 2 o'clock on Friday morning . . . when fifteen or twenty men, somewhat weary, are sitting around a table, [and] some one of them will say: 'Who will we nominate?'" After the convention George Harvey, a journalist and party powerhouse, asserted that Harding had been chosen by a cabal of fellow senators at an early-morning meeting held in a smoke-filled hotel room. But no one supported Harvey's account, and the next day most of the senators who had supposedly agreed to vote for Harding had continued to vote for other candidates through several more ballots. Until the very last ballot Harding received the votes of only three of the sixteen senators who were delegates to the convention.

The charge that Harding was a political stooge may be a canard. Murray insists that Harding resisted most of the importunate demands of friends when filling out his Cabinet and points out it included some of the best minds in the country, from Charles Evans Hughes to Andrew Mellon to Herbert Hoover. Murray also notes that when Harding became President, he decided, against the advice of his conservative allies, to pardon the controversial Socialist Eugene V. Debs, who had been sentenced to prison for sedition during World War I.

Harding knew he wasn't the brightest President. But he didn't

Legends, Lies, and Cherished Myths

pretend to be otherwise. William Allen White told how Harding was so perplexed by the lectures he'd been given on some tax measure that he virtually broke down and sobbed in front of one of his secretaries. "John, I can't make a damn thing out of this tax problem," Harding reportedly complained. "I listen to one side and they seem right, and then—God!—I talk to the other side and they seem just as right, and here I am where I started. I know somewhere there is a book that will give me the truth, but, hell, I couldn't read the book. I know somewhere there is an economist who knows the truth, but I don't know where to find him and haven't the sense to know him and trust him when I find him. God! what a job!"

He wasn't an accomplished writer. And as he himself liked to joke, he took great pleasure in "bloviating," giving rise to H. L. Mencken's charge that Harding's English "reminds me of a string of wet sponges. . . . It is a style that rolls and groans, struggles and complains. It is the style of a rhinoceros liberating himself by main strength from a lake of boiling molasses." But in the opinion of social historian Eric Goldman, Harding could write well when he tried. Goldman points out, "[I]n a curious irony, this Chief Executive generally deemed the least skillful with words anticipated the most famous sentence of the President usually considered particularly distinguished for the literary quality of his utterances. In Augusta [Georgia], President Harding said that he hoped the people of the South as well as of the North would 'think more of what you can do for your Government than of what your Government can do for you.' " And Harding did not, despite what everybody thinks, coin the word "normalcy." Goldman says it had "long been in legitimate if rare usage."

Finally, Harding didn't commit suicide and he wasn't murdered. He died of a heart attack, a not unusual circumstance in a fifty-seven-year-old man with a history of heart disease. The claim that he was poisoned was invented by Gaston Means, a former federal agent, who in the 1930's became infamous for swindling a woman out of a hundred thousand dollars "by promising," according to Harding biographer Francis Russell, "to put her in touch with a gang holding the Lindbergh baby, a gang existing solely in his imagination."[22]

Calvin Coolidge, when he is remembered at all, is remembered primarily for the jokes and stories told at his expense. Some recall the foolish statement he made in a column on unemployment: "When more and more people are thrown out of work, unemployment results." Others recount how he liked having his head rubbed with Vaseline at breakfast. And everybody remembers Dorothy Parker's famous line. After he died, she asked, "How can they tell?"

Even supporters, like the conservative Paul Johnson, haven't been able to resist parodying their hero. In a single paragraph Johnson quotes Alice Roosevelt Longworth's comment that Coolidge looked as if he'd been "weaned on a pickle," says Coolidge was "hatchet-faced," and tells how immediately after his wedding ceremony Coolidge gave his wife a bag of socks to darn. Coolidge has been considered so odd and so mediocre that even in his own lifetime nothing said about him seemed too farfetched. In his autobiography William Shirer recalls how in the Paris edition of the Chicago *Tribune* James Thurber, "unable to restrain himself," used to attribute the dumbest truisms to Coolidge—and get away with it. "Once," writes Shirer, "he had Coolidge addressing a convention of Protestant churches and proclaiming that a 'man who does not pray is not a praying man.'"

Coolidge was a character, but he was not dumb. A graduate of Amherst, he knew several languages and even translated Dante's *Inferno* into English in his spare time. He wrongly encouraged speculation on Wall Street and is therefore partly to blame for the crash. But historians consider him a shrewd operator who only liked to appear to be simple. Thomas Bailey says he was "a subtle master of self-advertising" and points out that although he rarely allowed himself to be quoted, Coolidge gave more interviews to the press than any other President before him.

He wasn't quiet, the fact that he was known as Silent Cal notwithstanding. Journalists Robert Ferrell and Howard Quint ac-

Legends, Lies, and Cherished Myths

tually call him the "talkative President." Press conference transcripts released after he died showed that when speaking "on background," he could be voluble. In public he appeared laconic because he felt it was better that way. He reportedly explained to Herbert Hoover, when Hoover was elected President, "If you don't say anything, you won't be called on to repeat it."

Despite his reputation for sternness, Coolidge liked to play practical jokes. One prank grew out of his discovery, after an early-morning walk, of an alarm button on the front porch of the White House. "Feigning he was tired," a Secret Service agent recalled, "he leaned against the button and pressed it. His solemn, immobile expression unchanged, he walked hurriedly into the house and from behind the safety of the living-room curtains peeked out and saw two policemen come tearing across the lawn, survey the scene, and, finding no one, return to the guard house. He pushed the button two more times and each time he would, without change of expression, watch the excitement that resulted."

At press conferences he proved he was not only well informed but witty. In one exchange with a reporter he confirmed that he was going to a fair the next day:

> REPORTER: It isn't likely you'll say anything tomorrow at the Fair?
> PRESIDENT: No. I am just going as an exhibit.

In another exchange Coolidge had this to say about some tariff questions: "I haven't had any report from the Tariff Commission on butter, or straw hats, or gold leaf. I have a report on cotton gloves."[23]

Herbert Hoover, like Calvin Coolidge, is an easy target for ridicule. In the 1928 election he made a lot of foolishly smug predictions about the economy, saying, "We in America today are nearer to the final triumph over poverty than ever before in the history of any land." At one point in 1930 he predicted unemployment would be eliminated within sixty days. In his memoirs he seriously asserted that people turned to selling apples in the 1930's because it was so "profitable."

But he can't fairly be accused of greeting news of the Depression with insouciance. From the moment the market crashed, Hoover became a whirlwind of activity. "Within days after the crash," according to biographer Gene Smith, "he held nine major conferences at the White House." Later he persuaded businessmen to cut profits instead of wages. Still not convinced he'd done enough, he asked Congress to lower taxes, asked the states to begin massive public works projects, and even recommended (albeit reluctantly) the establishment of the Reconstruction Finance Corporation, a harbinger of the New Deal. His efforts to restore the economy were so energetic and drastic that some have even called him the real father of the New Deal.

Hoover, one would have thought by now, should not need to be defended from the charge of inactivity. Yet so entrenched is the impression that he was a do-nothing President that even Republicans still believe it. When President Ronald Reagan seemed to ignore the stock market crash of 1987, Republicans urged him to "do something," so he wouldn't look like "another Hoover."[24]

Dwight Eisenhower, despite the testimony of supporters and the evidence of his own presidential papers, continues to be popularly regarded as a kind of political naïf. In fact, Ike was "a far more complex and devious man than most people realized," as Richard Nixon observed in *Six Crises*. Eisenhower's celebrated inarticulateness, for instance, was actually just a pose. In pre-press conference briefings, says historian Fred Greenstein, he told advisers which questions he planned to answer evasively. When he appeared at the podium, answers he wanted to fudge came out in typical Eisenhowerese, the "fuzzy locutions and opaque syntax" for which he was famous. Eisenhower privately used to brag that he was an accomplished wordsmith and pointed out it was he who had written some of General Douglas MacArthur's most memorable speeches when MacArthur served as military adviser to the Philippines in the 1930's.[25]

The fact that Earl Warren turned out to be a liberal Supreme Court justice is thought to have taken Eisenhower by surprise. Eisenhower let people think that. But he went ahead with the appointment even though he seems to have known from the beginning Warren would leave a liberal mark on the court. Bryce Harlow, a chief political adviser, told him at the time, "As Chief Justice, Mr. Warren's liberal philosophy will long influence the course of our government in directions reactionaries could hardly stomach. That liberal influence will be far greater now, as everyone—even a reactionary knows, than had Warren remained Governor of California."[26]

So established is the myth about Camelot that even today, according to the public opinion polls, John Kennedy is still one of the two or three most admired Presidents in the history of the United States. And no amount of evidence seems to convince people he was anything but admirable. Not the fact that he used women as sex objects, sleeping with hundreds of them, many of whom he couldn't even name (recalled one woman: "He was as compulsive as Mussolini. 'Up against the wall, Signora, if you have five minutes,' that sort of thing"); not even the fact that as President he possibly exposed himself to blackmail by sleeping with the girl friend of a known mobster. Greatness has been pinned on Kennedy like a rose that apparently won't wilt until a new generation that has no direct memory of him comes along.[27]

Given the known facts, one can only wonder how he managed to avoid a major scandal while he was alive. Even his war record was fraudulently inflated. When his PT-109 was cut in half by a destroyer during World War II, he rescued, according to historian Garry Wills, not three men as he claimed, but one man. Wills further charges that Kennedy deliberately falsified his account of the incident to conceal the fact that the disaster may have been caused by his own negligence. Kennedy always maintained that the little boat was split in two during an attack on a destroyer. Wills's interviews with members of Kennedy's crew indicate, however, that the PT-109 was rammed during a lull, when Kennedy and everybody else on board in effect were caught napping. "The destroyer loomed over the idling PT boat," says Wills, "before anyone knew it was near." From what's known about PT boats, one suspects this is the only way the mishap could have occurred. As Wills points out, the image of a little boat like the *PT-109's* being outmaneuvered and struck by a ponderous destroyer in the midst of a naval battle is mind-boggling.

Claims on behalf of Kennedy's major literary works stand up no better to sustained scrutiny than the discredited *PT-109* story. As it turns out, Kennedy's undergraduate thesis, *Why England Slept*, was based partly on research provided by political columnist Arthur Krock, a friend of Kennedy's rich father. The book received a terrific review in *The New York Times*, a review written by Krock himself.

The better-known *Profiles in Courage*, for which Kennedy received a Pulitzer Prize, was also prepared by others. According to biographer Herbert Parmet, it was organized by a Kennedy supporter, Jules Davids, and written by and large by Theodore Sorensen, one of Kennedy's speech writers.[28]

Ronald Reagan is responsible for one of the main myths about Ronald Reagan: that he always has been a conservative. Since he became a politician, Reagan has been adamant about this subject. When asked in the 1980's about his vigorous support of the Democratic party in 1932, he answered, "The Roosevelt that I voted for had promised to cut federal spending by 25 percent, had promised to return to the states and local communities authority and autonomy that had been unjustly seized by the federal government." In Reagan's eyes, Roosevelt himself was originally a conservative. "I looked up F.D.R.'s old platform," he told interviewers, "and I discovered that it called for a restoration of states' rights and a reduction in the national budget. You know what? I'm still for that." "I didn't desert my party," he said. "It deserted me."

In fact, not only did Reagan support Roosevelt in 1932, when he might have been misled by FDR's budget-balancing talk, but he also voted for Roosevelt in 1936, 1940, and 1944. "Indeed,"

Legends, Lies, and Cherished Myths

writes historian William Leuchtenburg, "Reagan's devotion to Roosevelt was greatest not in 1932, when F.D.R. made the pledge of slashing government spending, but after he had put through the precedent-smashing legislation that centralized authority in Washington." After Roosevelt died, Reagan continued to support Democrats and liberals. Liberals supported Harry Truman in 1948; so did Reagan. Liberals supported Hubert Humphrey's senatorial campaign in Minnesota; so did Reagan. Liberals supported Helen Gahagan Douglas over Richard Nixon in the 1950 Senate race in California; so did Reagan. Liberals dreamed of creating a world government to rid the world of war; so did Reagan, a member of the board of directors of the United World Federalists. When liberals founded the Americans for Democratic Action, Reagan helped put together a branch in California.

His record on the Communist witch-hunts is confusing. While he admitted confidentially to the FBI that he had been a member of a committee that was trying to "purge" Hollywood of Communists, in public hearings he indicated he didn't want to identify himself with the witch-hunters. After he had already been dismissed from the witness table during the congressional probe of Communist influence in Hollywood, he asked to make one further comment on the issue. While he detested the Communists' philosophy, "I never as a citizen want to see our country become urged, by either fear or resentment of this group, that we ever compromise with any of our democratic principles." In private, he told the FBI he wanted to see the Communist party outlawed; in public he said he opposed the effort. Which was the real Reagan is hard to establish. It may be he himself was unsure. All critics agree that it was about this time that he underwent a shift in views, from liberal to conservative. Leuchtenburg dates the change at about 1950, when Reagan began working as an official spokesman for General Electric; Garry Wills says the change occurred earlier, around 1947, when Reagan began to identify with Hollywood's moneyed interests.[29]

From Rags
to Riches

Those who are distressed to learn that many of the most popular beliefs about Presidents are false may be gratified to discover that at least there's truth to the old idea that anybody can grow up to be President. But not too much truth.

Of all our Presidents, only one or two started out dirt poor; the rest grew up in the middle class or higher, usually the latter. The great majority benefited from inherited advantages denied to most of their countrymen. By the reckoning of historian Edward Pessen, sixteen Presidents came from the upper class, another sixteen from the upper middle class, three from the middle class, and three from the lower middle class. Just one (Andrew Johnson) was out-and-out poor, unless you include Richard Nixon, as you conceivably could (though Pessen puts him in the lower-middle-class category).

Much of the confusion about the origins of the Presidents stems from the vague way in which the word "poor" is frequently used. Abraham Lincoln is almost universally believed to have been poor, and by modern standards he was. But he wasn't poor compared with his neighbors. According to Pessen, Lincoln's father belonged to the richest 15 percent of taxpayers in his community. Similarly, Lyndon Johnson is usually described as a son of poverty, and he himself gave people that impression. The description is only partly true. Although he grew up with poverty, he was hardly your average poor boy. His father was a state legislator; when Lyndon was growing up he was regarded as someone special because he was Sam Johnson's boy. When cotton prices were high, the family life-style was high, too.

Some of the confusion about the Presidents is due not to semantic vagueness but to deliberate lies. For example, the erroneous belief that William Henry Harrison was born poor was a fabrication of his campaign managers. He was actually born to a well-to-do plantation family; his father was a signer of the Declaration of Independence. Harrison's true background was considered an unfortunate liability in a presidential candidate and was conveniently suppressed.

Harrison's campaign marked the first in which such lies were told, but it was hardly the last. Later Grover Cleveland was described, as in a popular biography, as coming from "a poor and commonplace stock," although he really came from a long line of distinguished ministers. More recently Ronald Reagan has liked to claim his family was poor, but neighbors in Dixon, Illinois, where he spent his youth, remember the Reagans were far from starving. "They were not worse off than anybody [else]," said one. "Jack and Nell [father and mother] were always well dressed," said another. Garry Wills points out that during the harshest days of the Depression Ronald and his brother, Neil, went to college; both brothers finished school. When their father lost his job as a shoe salesman, the family endured hard times for several months, but eventually they were rescued when Jack Reagan got a job with a New Deal program. At a time when some people were starving, Jack Reagan owned a car.

At least Ronald Reagan can rightly claim he was self-made. Most Presidents can't.

George Washington: His great-grandfather was a member of Virginia's exclusive Royal Council. His father ran a plantation of ten thousand acres, complete with forty-nine slaves.

John Adams: His mother was a Boylston, one of the leading families of Massachusetts. His father virtually ran Braintree, the small town where Adams grew up.

Thomas Jefferson: Descended from a speaker of the House of Burgesses, he was reared in luxury. His father, Peter Jefferson, owned thousands of acres of rich Virginia farmland and was a member of the colonial legislature.

James Madison: His father owned five thousand acres of prime Virginia land and possessed more than a hundred slaves.

James Monroe: His mother came from a long line of distinguished Virginians, including a member of the House of Burgesses. When Monroe's father died, James was reared by his uncle, who served as the king's attorney for the colony and was a member of the legislature.

John Quincy Adams: For him the presidency was virtually a birthright. The Adams family was to nineteenth-century America what the Kennedys have been to the twentieth century (except that the Adamses didn't have half as much money as the Kennedys).

Andrew Jackson: Although he came from a less distinguished line than the first six Presidents, he was not born poor. At age fifteen, when his grandfather died, he inherited more than three hundred pounds.

Martin Van Buren: His father owned a tavern and five slaves and was considered a community leader.

William Henry Harrison: A member of the FFV (First Families of Virginia), his father inherited six plantations and was a legislator in the House of Burgesses.

John Tyler: Another member of the FFV, Tyler grew up on a twelve-hundred-acre estate with forty slaves. His father was governor of Virginia.

James K. Polk: His uncle was said to be the richest man in Mecklenburg County, North Carolina. Polk's father was a prosperous planter and once invested forty thousand dollars in a steamboat.

Legends, Lies, and Cherished Myths

Zachary Taylor: A *Mayflower* descendant, Taylor grew up on a ten-thousand-acre plantation with two dozen slaves.

Millard Fillmore: the first President born in a log cabin, he grew up in lower-middle-class circumstances.

Franklin Pierce: His father was a general in the Revolutionary War and later served as governor of New Hampshire.

James Buchanan: He grew up in a two-story brick house on a three-hundred-acre estate. His father was praised by contemporaries as "one of the most prominent citizens" in the county.

Abraham Lincoln: Though he lived in a cabin with a dirt floor, he did not grow up dirt poor—or at least not as dirt poor as his neighbors.

Andrew Johnson: Here was the only President, insists Pessen, who was born poor.

Ulysses S. Grant: Although he lived in poverty as an adult, he was born to a prosperous family. His father was said to be the richest man in the small town in Ohio in which Grant grew up.

Rutherford B. Hayes: He grew up in luxury with the help of his maternal uncle, a partner in the largest merchandising house in Cleveland.

James A. Garfield: Though he often claimed he was born poor, the Garfield family, biographers have noted, never had to take charity and was always well fed.

Chester A. Arthur: His family was never well off, but his father, a minister, graduated from college at a time when few Americans even finished high school.

Grover Cleveland: His father graduated from Yale University; after his father died, Grover lived with his uncle, reputedly one of the richest men in Buffalo.

Benjamin Harrison: He was the grandson of President William Henry Harrison.

William McKinley: His father was a prosperous manufacturer.

Theodore Roosevelt: Born into the New York aristocracy, his father inherited a million dollars.

William Howard Taft: His father inherited a hundred thousand dollars and later became attorney general of the United States.

Woodrow Wilson: His father was a Princeton graduate who later became a minister. While never rich, the family lived in a large brick house complete with stables and a garden.

Warren G. Harding: His grandfather built the largest house in the community. Harding's father was less successful but was still no failure.

Calvin Coolidge: His father had an annual income of only fifteen hundred dollars, but he managed to save up twenty-five thousand dollars over his lifetime and served, appropriately, on the board of directors of a local bank.

Herbert Hoover: Orphaned at the age of eight, he was brought up by his maternal uncle, the head of a local academy.

Franklin D. Roosevelt: The young FDR's prospects seemed so assured that a jaded Grover Cleveland warned Roosevelt never to seek the presidency.

Harry S. Truman: While never wealthy, his parents did well enough. His mother inherited a farm worth $150,000; his father earned $15,000 a year.

Dwight David Eisenhower: His mother had attended college; his father ran a 160-acre farm he received as a wedding gift.

John F. Kennedy: His father was so rich that he accumulated a fortune estimated at about a hundred million dollars in the 1930's; before World War II ended, his father was worth twice as much.

Lyndon B. Johnson: He was the son of a state legislator.

Richard M. Nixon: His father owned a gas station.

Gerald R. Ford: His stepfather ran a prosperous paint business.

Jimmy Carter: His father was the classic big fish in a small pond. A member of the state legislature, Carter's father also ran a prosperous farm.[1]

Related to the belief that Presidents were frequently born poor is the idea that many grew up in log cabins. The evidence is against the proposition. William Henry Harrison, of hard cider and log cabin fame, grew up in a sturdy, even elegant two-and-a-half-story red-brick mansion, complete with dormered windows and a good

Legends, Lies, and Cherished Myths

wide view of the James River. Andrew Johnson, poor though he was, wasn't born in a log cabin either, despite the statement to the contrary by at least one of his biographers. According to more thorough researchers, Johnson was born in a "small frame house, with a shingled gambrel roof, having an outside stone and brick chimney." Johnson's successor, Ulysses S. Grant, likewise was born in a frame house, though millions were led to believe otherwise. The error was memorialized in 1922, when the federal government issued a half-dollar with Grant's face on one side and a small log cabin on the other. Literature distributed with the coin claimed Grant had been born in a log cabin.*

The practice of linking Presidents to log cabins is less popular now than in years past, but it endures. It has been most forcefully advanced in recent times by Dr. Norman Vincent Peale. Peale's belief is that the log cabin birth is ennobling. His main evidence relates to the log cabin birth of Abraham Lincoln, which is said to account for Lincoln's greatness. "God knows how to do things," says Peale. "When, for example, He wanted to bring up the greatest man in all the long history of the American people, where did He have him born? In one of the great and wealthy homes of the nation? Not at all! He had him born in Kentucky, in a mud-plastered, windowless cabin, the beams of which were hewn out of the frontier."

Peale does not explain what went wrong with John Wilkes Booth, Lincoln's killer, who shared the presumed advantage of a log cabin birth. Maybe his came with a window.[2]

Presidents aside, it's widely believed that businessmen have frequently gone from rags to riches, though the evidence shows they more likely went from rich to richer. Of the top two hundred business leaders in the country at the turn of the century, Herbert Gutman reports, 95 percent came from middle- or upper-class families. Andrew Carnegie, who is always held up as an example of the rags-to-riches phenomenon, was an exception.

*Grant once did live in a log cabin he made with the help of his friends, but that was long after he had grown up and left the wood-frame home of his childhood.

63
From Rags to Riches

True believers in the myth need not despair entirely. There is plenty of evidence Americans have made it from rags to middle-class respectability in considerable numbers.[3] Gutman says he found that poor boys in the nineteenth century frequently became the heads of middle-size businesses. *

Most Americans who were rich in the nineteenth century, of course, had been born rich. In the era of Jackson, according to studies by Pessen, only 2 percent of the urban elite ascended from poverty; only 6 percent came out of the middle class.

There weren't many rich folks around then, but they owned a vastly disproportionate amount of the country's wealth. ** In 1828 the richest 4 percent of the population of New York City owned about half the wealth there. By 1845 the rich had become even richer, and a mere 1 percent of the city's population owned almost half its wealth. It took the rest of the country a little time to catch up, but by the Civil War most American cities showed similar patterns of concentrated wealth. "In Baltimore, New Orleans, and St. Louis," writes Pessen, "the richest one per cent of the population owned about two-fifths, the richest five per cent better than two-thirds, and the upper ten per cent more than four-fifths of the wealth."

Americans were supposed to be living in near-perfect equality then. During this period Alexis de Tocqueville made his famous observation that the most novel thing about the United States was the "equality of conditions." In fact, the only time conditions had been anything like equal was before the Revolution. If ever there was an Age of the Common Man, it was in the period when we were still ruled by Britain. As one scholar discovered, in prerevolutionary Boston, New York, and Philadelphia about a third of the elite had been born poor. By Jackson's day the era of the self-made rich man was about over.[4]

That Americans have always wanted to be rich is usually taken

*There's some question about how to define "middle class." Gutman describes a poor boy named Watson who wound up owning a business which employed eleven hundred people and calls him middle class. Some might disagree, one man's middle class being another man's upper class.
**There were so few rich people then that they could comfortably have fitted into a small ballroom. In the early 1830's only a hundred or so New Yorkers were worth more than a hundred thousand dollars; just seventy-five were worth that much in Boston. There were hardly any millionaires.

for granted by people who can't imagine that anyone would want to be poor or merely middle-class. In fact, for centuries Americans were uncomfortable with wealth, so much so that down to the Revolution the presence of wealth was often regarded as a cause for alarm. David Hackett Fischer, commenting on this phenomenon, says that "from John Winthrop to John Adams, Americans thanked God that they were not a wealthy nation, for they believed that wealth spawned luxury and corruption and despotism and all the other ugly things that the Old World allegedly was and the New World wasn't—yet."

Much as people may think they really believe in wealth, there's reason to suspect they're uncomfortable with it. Long after Americans had turned in the nineteenth century to the worship of millionaires, they continued to glorify the poor. Thus greed for the riches of John D. Rockefeller and Henry Ford persisted oddly, right along with the celebration of Lincoln's alleged poverty. Even today, as John Kenneth Galbraith has pointed out, it is considered somewhat embarrassing to be rich, as is evident from the way the rich have to shroud their true political intentions. "There is, it is clear, a basic asymmetry in our political discourse," he writes. "One can be for help to the poor—the hungry, the homeless, those without jobs or prospects. But one cannot be publicly for a policy on behalf of the rich. We have such policies; they are a wholly predictable aspect of our political alignments; it is only that they may not be admitted. The rich in our time have become a dirty secret. There must be that cover story, however improbable."

Claims on behalf of the poor are limited, however. While the poor have our sympathy, no one wants to be poor. And today no one thinks poverty is a great molder of character, as people once believed. Poverty, as the muckrakers first showed at the turn of the century and as everyone now realizes, is a distinct liability and a great breeder of crime and corruption.

Ever since the muckrakers, Americans have ably, though not entirely, resisted the monkish appeals of poverty. Lincoln's poverty still stirs the imagination. Few Americans seem willing to admit that Lincoln, as one early-twentieth-century editor observed, be-

From Rags to Riches

came great not because of poverty but despite it. Americans prefer to think the business about Lincoln's long walks to school and other such sacrifices contributed somehow to his later success.[5]

Perhaps Lincoln's foot calluses had something to do with it. Success never seems to come but through hard work, often physically demanding work at that. Pure luck doesn't seem to play a role.

Except in real life, of course—and in the novels written by Horatio Alger, though hardly anyone remembers that. While most people identify Alger with the conventional rags-to-riches myth, the fact that most of his heroes achieve success only through luck is conveniently overlooked. In the typical Alger novel, the down-on-his-luck street urchin happens to rescue a drowning child or foil a robbery, a fact that brings him to the fortuitous attention of a wealthy patron, who "at once rewards him with a handsome gift of money to finance his first steps upward to fame and fortune," as historian R. Richard Wohl has brought out. In *Ragged Dick* the hero gets his big break during a ferryboat ride taken on a holiday from work. A little boy slips off the deck into the water below. His father, who can't swim, screams for help. "My child. Who will save my child? A thousand—ten thousand dollars to any one who will save him." Dick instantly jumps in and saves the boy. The father, who turns out to be a rich merchant, rewards Dick with money, new clothes, and a good-paying job. At the end of the novel Ragged Dick, now on his way to fame and fortune, takes on a new name commensurate with his new prospects, Richard Hunter, Esq. He next appears, as Wohl points out, in Alger's sequel, *Fame and Fortune.*[6]

Sex

The subject of sex may be the most fertile source of myths in American history. Of these, the chief one is probably the firmly held belief that premarital sex is a twentieth-century phenomenon.

Plainly, premarital sex has been more widely practiced in this century than ever before. But prenuptial copulating wasn't exactly conceived in the sexually promiscuous days of the 1960's or in the sultry days of Prohibition, when young people drunk on bootleg gin whooped it up in the rumble seats of their daddies' sedans.

As it turns out, Americans have a history of lustiness. Evidence indicates that Americans had healthy carnal appetites even back in colonial times, when sex supposedly was practiced only by husbands and wives who wanted children. In Bristol, Rhode Island, for example, between 1720 and 1740, one out of ten wives gave birth within the first eight months of marriage. During the next twenty years almost one out of every two newlywed couples had a baby before their marriage was nine months old. In venerable Concord, Massachusetts, a third of all babies born in the twenty years before the Revolution were conceived out of wedlock.[1]

One group of colonial Americans is believed to have been more puritanical than the rest: the Puritans. If Americans are sure of anything, it is that the Puritans were hostile to sex, and, for that matter, all other worldly pleasures as well. As H. L. Mencken put it in 1925, Puritanism amounted to the "haunting fear that someone, somewhere, may be happy."[2]

Actually the only "haunting fear" may be that Americans will never learn the truth about the Puritans and will forever misunderstand them. Scholars long ago determined that while the Puritans frowned on immorality and were no doubt less promiscuous than their descendants, they happily welcomed the practice of sex. When one married couple revealed that they had been abstaining from sex to achieve a higher spirituality, John Cotton, the Puritan's Puritan, sternly recorded his belief that they were the victims of "blind zeal," adding, "They are the dictates of a blind mind that follow therein, and not of the Holy Spirit, which saith, *It is not good that man should be alone.*"

Some have charged that the Puritans were sexually repressed and inhibited, supposedly the reason for Americans' long-standing hang-ups about sex. In reality the Puritans not only considered intercourse within marriage a positive good but talked about it in public. When one James Mattock refused to sleep with his wife for two years running, the matter was taken up by the members of his congregation at the First Church of Boston. After a free and open discussion of the subject they expelled him.

In some ways Puritan families may have been even more open about sex than American families today. As historian Jerry Frost points out, given the fact that parents and children usually lived together in the same room, they really had no choice. Even if parents had been inclined to conceal the rudimentary facts of sex from their children, as a practical matter they couldn't.[3]

As a matter of fact, the Puritans apparently didn't try very hard to shelter their children from sex and may have been less protective than parents are now. Today not even liberal parents allow their teenage daughters to sleep with potential suitors. But the Puritans did—as long as everyone remained clothed. The practice, known as bundling, sometimes led to sexual experimentation and unwanted babies. Nonetheless, it flourished.[4]

The strongest charges leveled against the Puritans—that they punished sex offenders brutally—is exaggerated. Most adulterers, for instance, got off with just a whipping and a fine. In all of seventeenth-century Massachusetts only three adulterers were ever put to death. Says Edmund Morgan: "Sodomy, to be sure, they usually punished with death; but rape, adultery, and fornication they regarded as pardonable human weaknesses, all the more likely to appear in a religious community, where the normal course of sin was stopped by wholesome laws."[5]

The Puritans did ostracize certain sexual offenders but usually allowed transgressors to continue to play a role in the community. According to Carl Degler, confessed fornicators were even allowed to remain members of the church. Some, of course, suffered badly, but few had to undergo the ordeal of wearing the letter A (for adultery) as Hester Prynne did in Nathaniel Hawthorne's *The Scarlet Letter.* *

The Puritans were not as open-minded about sexual immorality as Americans are today, of course, but they weren't as closed-minded as many of the moralists, like Anthony Comstock, who came later. As the historian Carl Degler observes, "The Sabbatarian, antiliquor, and antisex attitudes usually attributed to the Puritans are a nineteenth-century addition to the much more moderate and wholesome view of life's evils held by the early settlers of New England." In any case, the Puritans were no more morally intolerant than other religious groups that settled in America in the 1600's. To single them out as somehow different is simply unfair.[6]

The Puritans, of course, aren't the only Americans who've been maligned for their views on sex. So have the Victorians.

* Some people think that Hawthorne's use of the letter A was merely an invention of his own making. It was not. In 1636 New Plymouth enacted a law that required adulterers "to weare two Capitall letters viz. AD. cut out in cloth and sowed on theire uper most Garments on theire arm or backe." (See Claude M. Simpson, ed., *The Centenary Edition of the Works of Nathaniel Hawthorne* [1972], p. 618.)

To be sure, Victorians—women especially—often seemed prudish. Captain Frederick Marryat, an English traveler, recalled meeting a schoolteacher who was so straitlaced she dressed the legs of her classroom piano "in modest little trousers with frills at the bottom of them." Mark Twain's wife was so prudish she felt it necessary to bowdlerize her husband's prose. So did Nathaniel Hawthorne's wife. After Hawthorne died, she systematically went through all his diaries and love letters to make sure they were completely spotless. In one place she even changed "got into bed" to "composed myself to sleep," to avoid the suggestive nature of the word "bed." In another place she expunged the word "bosom" in connection with the description of an Egyptian mummy. Occasionally, when blocking out the offensive words with ink didn't seem sufficient, she used scissors to cut them out.[7]

All the same, there's plenty of evidence that the mere mention of sex didn't bother many Victorians at all. Millions bought marriage handbooks that were as sexually explicit as manuals available today. The author of one handbook, Frederick Hollick, insisted that women should have orgasms just as men did. When intercourse is performed properly, he wrote, "both beings are thrown into a species of mental ecstasy and bodily fever, during which all other thoughts and functions are totally suspended, and all the vital forces are concentrated in the Reproductive system."

The stereotypical Victorian woman, of course, is thought to have been so repressed she never even thought about sex. As Dr. William Acton put it at the time, "The *best* mothers, wives, and managers of households know little or nothing of sexual indulgence. Love of home, children, and domestic duties are the only passions that they feel."

But as it turns out, while Victorian women were probably far less promiscuous than those who came before and later, they did think about sex. When Dr. Clelia Mosher surveyed the sexual attitudes of forty-five middle-class housewives in the 1890's, she discovered that most had strong opinions about the subject. Most of the women—the majority of whom had been born before 1870—even admitted experiencing orgasms.

More revealing, in light of the popular belief that Victorians engaged in sex only for making babies, was that most of the women professed to believe in the sake of sex for sex alone. One woman, born before 1850, said she considered the sexual "appetite as ranking with other natural appetites and like them to be indulged legitimately and temperately." Another woman, born before 1861, said that "the desire of both husband and wife for this expression of their union seems to me the first and highest reason for intercourse. The desire for offspring is a secondary, incidental, although entirely worthy motive."

Whether Mosher's survey was representative is unknown. But even many moralists conceded that men and women were apt to indulge in sex for pleasure despite all the speeches made against it. As physician John Knowles sadly put it, "there will be many, the vast majority, perhaps, who will not bring their minds to accept the truth which nature seems to teach, which would confine sexual acts to Reproduction alone."[8]

In fact, the average Victorian seems to have had a hard time living up to a lot of the moral standards established to guarantee his rectitude. Prostitution became so prevalent after the Civil War that officials in several cities considered giving it legal status. In 1867 the New York City Police Department endorsed a plan to regulate the trade. In St. Louis, until church leaders intervened, prostitution was legally recognized.

In the boom cities out West miners and railroad workers used the services of so many prostitutes that brothels became an important part of the local economy. In old Sandy, Utah, almost the entire community was devoted to servicing nearby miners, who wanted a convenient place to drink and copulate.

In the big cities in the East prostitution was practiced so openly that thick guidebooks were published to direct customers to the best whorehouses. The author of one guidebook, *The Gentleman's Directory*, explained the purpose was to give the reader from out of town "an insight into the character and doings of people whose deeds are carefully screened from public view; when we describe their houses, and give their location, we supply the stranger with information of which he stands in need, we supply a void that otherwise must remain unfilled. Not that we imagine the reader will ever desire to visit these houses. Certainly not; he is, we do not doubt, a member of the Bible Society, a bright and shining light, like Newful Gardner or John Allen. But we point out the location of these places in order that the reader may know how to avoid them."[9]

Everything is always supposed to get better and better in America, but under Victorianism prostitution seemed to go from bad to worse. It's been estimated that in New York in 1870 there were roughly ten thousand whores. Twenty years later the police commissioner estimated the number at forty thousand. No one knows precisely how many prostitutes actually roamed the streets then since the idea of measuring the trade scientifically had not yet occurred to anybody. When a reliable survey was undertaken in New York just before World War I, investigators concluded there were far fewer whores than people had imagined, but still quite enough: fifteen thousand.[10]

Most Victorians, whatever they did behind closed doors, seemed to have approved of the moral crusade which defined the age. But not everyone did. It's worth remembering that this period, which gave us the mail-censoring Anthony Comstock and the book-banning New England Watch and Ward Society, also produced the free love movement. Free lovers were a distinct minority, but they enjoyed surprising support throughout the country. Victoria Woodhull, one of the most radical advocates of free love, was in constant demand as a public lecturer. People came despite her extreme statements, which included a frontal attack on conventional marriage. When asked about her own morality once, she snapped: "If I want sexual intercourse with one or one hundred men I shall have it . . . and this sexual intercourse business may as well be discussed now, and discussed until you are so familiar with your sexual organs that a reference to them will no longer make the blush mount to your face any more than a reference to any other part of your body."[11]

The fact is even mainstream Victorians were more broad-

Legends, Lies, and Cherished Myths

minded about sex than is often popularly thought. As Grover Cleveland discovered, most people were willing to overlook indiscretions by major public figures. Though his reputation suffered, Cleveland was elected President after admitting he had sired a child out of wedlock.

And one suspects, though it's hard to prove, that many people must have grown tired of the moralizing even if they tried to live their own lives purely. Many writers became so annoyed with the official spirit of rectitude that they began mocking morality. In a speech, "The Science of Onanism," given before the so-called Stomach Club of Paris, Mark Twain satirized both Victorian oratorical style and moral taboos:

> All great writers upon health and morals, both ancient and modern, have struggled with this stately subject; this shows its dignity and importance. Some of these writers have taken one side, some the other. Homer, in the second book of the *Illiad*, says with fine enthusiasm, "Give me masturbation or give me death." Caesar, in his *Commentaries*, says, "To the lonely it is company; to the forsaken it is a friend; to the aged and the impotent it is a benefactor; they that are penniless are yet rich, in that they still have this majestic diversion." In another place this experienced observer has said, "There are times when I prefer it to sodomy."

In closing, Twain added: "I say, 'If you *must* gamble away your lives sexually, don't play a Lone Hand too much.' When you feel a revolutionary uprising in your system, get your Vendrôme Column down some other way—don't jerk it down."[12]

The mirror opposite of Victorianism was supposed to be the Roaring Twenties, when immorality replaced morality, Capone replaced Comstock, and everybody—until 1929, that is—had a good time.

In reality, the twenties probably didn't mark as big a shift in American morals as people think. To judge by the novels of William Dean Howells, the bonds of conventional morality may have begun slipping as early as the 1890's. If anything, the biggest changes may have appeared in the decade or two prior to World War I, not afterward. Historian Kenneth Lynn has pointed out that Theodore Dreiser's novels about philandering businessmen began being published in the early 1900's, and Ernest Hemingway's Nick Adams "lost his virginity well before a wartime spirit of eat, drink, and be merry allegedly infected the sex habits of America's young men."

It's true that newspapers in the twenties were filled with a lot more stories about sex than they had been before, but that was apparently only because Kent Cooper, a new general manager at the Associated Press, decided to expand the definition of news. If there was a revolution, then, it may have simply been a revolution in the American newspaper, not in American morals.

The revolution, whenever it began, is supposed to have ended promptly in 1930 with the onset of the Great Depression, which is regarded as a kind of punishment for a decade of orgies. As journalist Frederick Lewis Allen puts it in his ever-popular history of the period, *Only Yesterday*, the sexual revolution "had at last reached an armistice."

History didn't happen that way, however, except in Allen's own mind. At least, according to Lynn, there's no evidence of it. It is also plainly too Calvinistically neat. It's too easy to suggest that the Depression, like a cold shower, sobered up a people who had gone wild. As Lynn notes, Allen's analysis seems to tell more about Allen, the son of the founder of the New England Watch and Ward Society, than it did about America.[13]

Sex myths abound not only about certain decades but about certain places. One of the places most commonly mythologized is small-town America, considered a sanctuary of chaste morality, especially in the late nineteenth century. In fact, many children who grew up in small towns in the 1880's later recalled that the places were often immoral. Iowan Herbert Quick reported feeling that he had "more evil associates" out on the prairie than he probably ever would have had in the city. Quick marveled that he had somehow emerged from the heartland experience without any

Legends, Lies, and Cherished Myths

"scorching of the garments," so hot was the "fiery furnace" he walked through as a teenager. Kansan William Allen White recollected that as a boy he got an education in sex just walking down the street, reading the "Saxon words chalked on sidewalks and barns."[14]

Their testimony may not be conclusive, but it stands as a good reminder of the possibility that even the most familiar subjects can be complicated. History can be tricky. And it can be at its trickiest when it concerns a subject with which we are all familiar.

Consider the question of abortion. Everyone knows abortion is legal today only because of the famous Supreme Court decision in 1973. But the assumption of most people that before the Court's ruling abortion had always been illegal in the United States is wrong.

In fact, there were no laws in the United States against abortion until the 1820's. And for many years after that, most states permitted abortions in the first four months of pregnancy. Abortion began to be generally outlawed only in the mid-nineteenth century. Again, on the basis of the way the debate is shaped today, one would expect the clergy to have been behind the movement to outlaw abortion. But it was the medical profession that pushed for the change. Doctors undertook the effort after discovering with the help of the microscope that babies developed when an egg was fertilized by sperm. Before the discovery only the sperm had been detected; no one had seen an egg. "Thus," says Carl Degler, "what is spoken of today as the moment of conception, the time when egg and sperm unite, had no specific meaning or even conceptualization for people at the opening of the 19th century. About all that physicians and lay people alike knew was that at some point after sexual intercourse the male sperm (or egg) began to develop into a recognizably potential human being." As a result, everyone had believed that life began at about four months, when the mother felt the baby move in her stomach (a moment known as quickening).

Another common error about abortions is that they were uncommon until recently. Hard numbers are difficult to come by, but one researcher has estimated that in the second half of the nineteenth century there was one abortion for every half dozen or so births. In the 1920's, it's reported, about one in four pregnancies ended in an abortion.

Doctors railed against abortion, one lamenting that "even among the married, there are few wives who do not know of some means to destroy the foetus before it comes to full term, and who have not in some manner, and at some time, applied one or more of these means in their own cases." But women continued having abortions apparently because they provided a guaranteed method of birth control.

Abortions during all this time were generally illegal. Yet Americans seem not to have been terribly bothered by the widespread resort to the practice. One statistic is particularly revealing: Between 1849 and 1858 in Massachusetts, of thirty-two accused abortionists brought to trial, not one was convicted; juries composed solely of men freed every one of the suspects.

Women seemed even less inclined than men to condemn abortion. As one doctor sadly observed in 1896, "Many otherwise good and exemplary women, who would rather part with their right hands or let their tongues cleave to the roof of the mouth than to commit a crime, seem to believe that prior to quickening it is no more harm to cause the evacuation of the contents of their wombs than it is that of their bladders or their bowels."[15]

The Family

Fundamental to the mythology of
the American family is the idea that it can be conceived of as a
fixed institution. Historians insist that over the years the American
family has taken on numerous shapes and undergone radical
changes. To the man on the street, however, it is always just the
"good old American family," as if it has always remained the same,
like something out of a Norman Rockwell painting or television's
Leave It to Beaver.

There is the assumption, for instance, that child rearing has
always been left up to mothers. But according to recent studies of
the family undertaken by Stanford University's Carl Degler, child
rearing in colonial times was mainly the job of fathers. Until the
early 1800's child-rearing manuals were not even addressed to
mothers. It wasn't until the nineteenth century, when women had
the economic freedom to devote themselves full-time to their
offspring, that they began playing their familiar hearth and
home role.[1]

Children as well as parents in the colonial era played a markedly different role in the family from now. Regarded as little adults, children were made to dress like their parents, were given heavy responsibilities, and were forbidden the luxury of playthings. A historian who has studied 330 portraits of children between 1670 and 1810 discovered that until the Revolution the pictures "contain no distinctive childish artifacts such as toys, children's furniture, or school books. The stock poses give no signs of play or playfulness, and the faces of the children are as solemn as those of their elders." Until the 1800's children weren't even given books at their own reading levels; juvenile literature hadn't been invented. As late as 1845 the *Southern Literary Messenger* considered juvenile books a novelty. "No trait in the literary development of the age," said the *Messenger*, "is more striking than the importance which seems suddenly to have attached to what we call juvenile books for children."

Far from maintaining close relations with their children, parents in the seventeenth and eighteenth centuries often kept their offspring at bay. Puritan clergymen specifically urged parents not to become too close to their children. When male children reached their teens, they were often sent away to live with other families. When parents were divorced, the custody of the children was often considered a minor matter, according to Degler. Not until the nineteenth century did children become sentimentalized idols. Only then did families begin celebrating children's birthdays.[2]

Early colonial families revered the elderly, but Victorians did not. Reverence for the elderly began declining as early as the 1750's. By then children were openly defying their elders' authority. The head of the Carter clan in Virginia became so alarmed by his son's rebelliousness that he practically feared for his life. "Surely it is happy our laws prevent parricide," he wrote, "or the devil that moves to this treatment, would move to put his father out of the way. Good God! That such a monster is descended from my loins."

After the Revolution the elderly so often became the target of abuse that a whole vocabulary of scorn for them was developed. David Hackett Fischer has identified more than a dozen terms that came into use around this time to disparage the old, including "old cornstalk," "old goat," "geezer," "baldy," and "oldster." And according to Fischer, at the same time that these words appeared, others carrying positive connotations—"progenitor," "eldern," "beldam," "grandame," "grandsire," "forefather," "gramfer," "granther," and "granam"—began disappearing.[3]

Couples have been marrying for love for a long time, but not before 1750. According to Degler, not until then did magazines begin emphasizing that romantic love was at the "heart of an ideal marriage." Further, not until then did couples begin considering the loss of love a reason for divorce. "Prior to 1770," says Degler, "not a single one of the dozens of divorce proceedings in Massachusetts mentioned loss of affection as a ground for the separation of partners. But during the last twenty-five years of the century, some 10 percent of 121 suits for divorce named loss of affection as a ground."

No one knows precisely why the American family began undergoing as many changes as it did when it did—between 1750 and 1800—but apparently the transformation had to do with the increase in women's autonomy, which was made possible by the birth of industrialism and the rise of the cities. Change didn't come about evenly, however. As Degler notes, the "majority of families of the nation" did not undergo a major metamorphosis "until the opening of the twentieth century."

As if they were trying to make up for not believing in such radical changes in family life over the centuries, Americans believe firmly in other changes that never took place. One often hears that colonial Americans lived primarily in extended families, but scholars like John Demos have established "that small and essentially nuclear families were standard from the very beginning of American history." Once a couple married, they were encouraged to move immediately into a new home of their own. Frequently the bridegroom's family had to promise to help the couple find new accommodations as a condition of marriage. About the only time two generations lived together in the colonial era was when the elders became so old they couldn't care for themselves.

The pattern continued into the twentieth century, even among European immigrants. Degler reports that only about 25 percent of nineteenth-century immigrants lived in extended families.

Another belief is that colonial Americans married much younger than people do today. In reality, demographic studies have now proved that they usually married in their mid to late twenties, just as now. So much for all the chatter about the delays in marriage supposedly brought on by the complications of modern life. It appears that Americans have a tradition of marrying late. Going to college and starting a career have little to do with the matter.[4]

A major theme of popular sociology is that the family today is suffering from unprecedented problems. Families, to be sure are under stress. But many of the failings associated with the family in the 1980's have been misunderstood and exaggerated.

Most worrisome, of course, is the high rate of divorce. To judge by the comments of Ronald Reagan, the first divorced President, even those who have gone through with it are alarmed that so many others have as well. There's plenty about which to be alarmed. The American divorce rate is the worst in the world. Americans divorce four times as often as the British and three times as often as the French.

But divorce is not exactly a recent problem. In the late nineteenth century so many Americans divorced that the federal government decided it was a major social problem and undertook a study of the matter. In the 1880's there were twenty-five thousand divorces a year, more divorces than in any other industrialized country. By the 1920's, says Degler, Americans were divorcing almost as often as in the early 1960's.

In any case, the increase in the divorce rate over the past century may not mean that marriages are worse but only that Americans are more willing now—and more able—to bring unhappy marriages to an end. As historian Bernard Weisberger has pointed out, "Women are more ready to divorce bad husbands when they can get jobs; men are more willing to divorce if they are making enough to pay alimony and child support and also support themselves and maybe a new family. Prior to that, the only alternative was desertion—'the poor man's divorce.' "

The fact is, despite the high rate of divorce, marriage remains as popular as ever, and proportionately more Americans get married nowadays than ever before. Just a century ago a full 10 percent of American women refused to marry. In late-nineteenth-century Massachusetts 18 percent of the female population over fifty had never married. Today, however, almost everybody marries.

Marriages are probably under more stress today than earlier. This probably stems from the increasing autonomy of women, a development that began a long time ago. Court records show that the number of divorces began increasing in the nineteenth century, when women began demanding to be treated as equals. Men started filing for divorce in large numbers when their wives refused to subordinate their own interests to their husbands'. One husband in the 1870's even won a divorce because his wife refused to serve him breakfast.

Americans who are alarmed by the rising divorce rate often see it as a sign of a long-feared moral cataclysm brought on by the loss of old values and the failure of personal character. But the divorce rate has zigged and zagged so fast and so far throughout American history it hardly seems reasonable to assign moral weight to it. In the 1920's it went up for a time; in the thirties it leveled off; in the forties, after the war, it went up again, before going down again in the fifties. It is hard to believe that morality has followed the same path. The dramatic rise in divorces after World War II, for example, seems directly tied to the willingness of couples to end marriages hastily entered into during the conflict. It seems to have had little to do with any decline in morality.[5]

Critics may say that even if the divorce rate doesn't spring from a failure of national character, it has resulted in an unprecedented proliferation of single-parent homes. This just isn't true, however. Children in America have often had to grow up in single-parent families. In late-seventeenth-century Virginia, for instance, parents died so young that most children, during part of their growing years, were reared by just one parent, and more than a third lost both parents. In the nineteenth century death came so early that the proportion of families headed by a single parent was roughly the same as today. "It is quite true," says Degler, "that the ending of a marriage by death is different in many ways from an ending occasioned by divorce. Yet both have two important things in common. Both leave children with only a single parent, at least temporarily; both result in widespread incidence of combined or 'blended' families." Such families are not new.[6]

Americans idealize the families of the past and fear the worst for present families. The facts show, however, that divorce is not unique to our times, single-parent homes are not solely the creatures of modernity, and since colonial times American families have changed repeatedly.

War

Every July Fourth Americans say they like revolution. But it's best not to take them too seriously. They don't really mean it.

What they like is the American Revolution. Only they're under the impression the American Revolution wasn't really a revolution at all. Real revolution is bloody and fearful. Ours is believed to have been more like a tea party—a Boston Tea Party. As the Daughters of the American Revolution explained, in a pamphlet issued to aliens who might be misled into taking our rhetoric seriously, "A revolution usually means an attempt to tear down or overturn a government or wreck the existing institutions of a country. The American Revolution did none of these things."[1]

To be sure, the American Revolution was different from the other great modern upheavals in France, Russia, and China—but not as different as people think. As the historian Crane Brinton has observed, there was "more than the touch of the reign of terror" in the American conflict.

The extent of the barbarism can be measured in the treatment of loyalists, the Americans who stayed true to the king. They were not treated well. Countless loyalists were tarred and feathered. Thousands were forced to turn over millions of dollars in property without compensation. More than eighty thousand were driven to flee for safety to Canada, where many spent the remainder of their lives in poverty. One scholar has calculated that the American Revolution even produced more émigrés than the French Revolution: twenty-four émigrés per thousand of the population, compared with five per thousand for France.* [2]

The loyalists, of course, are seldom mentioned because they lost, and America is not terribly fond of losers—especially losers who didn't amount to much of an opposition. And in popular lore never was there a more useless opposition than the loyalists. Two hundred years later they are practically invisible. Children are taught that the war pitted Americans against foreigners in a classic battle for self-determination. The loyalists are rarely even mentioned.

Of all the nonsense spread about the Revolution, this is the most preposterous. The Revolutionary War actually pitted American against American and sometimes, as in the case of Benjamin Franklin, father against son. Only a minority of the people supported the Revolution; John Adams estimated about a third of the population was actually hostile to the idea; another third, indifferent.

The belief that loyalist opposition to the Revolution constituted an insignificant threat to the cause is widespread but spurious. Loyalists played a major role in the war. One statistic is telling: Almost as many Americans fought for Britain as fought against Britain. In 1780, when there were nine thousand patriots in Washington's army, eight thousand loyalists served in the British Army. [3]

Unlike the loyalist, the minuteman is well remembered—unfortunately not very accurately. It is widely believed that the minuteman who came to the defense of his country in its greatest hour of need was drawn from the ranks of the middle class. As Ralph

* But if we exiled more people, the French killed more. Some forty thousand people died in the French Revolution.

Legends, Lies, and Cherished Myths

Waldo Emerson put it, in commemorating Concord, "Here once the embattled farmers stood,/And fired the shot heard round the world."

This very comforting belief has little foundation in fact. While Americans like to think it was the average fellow who came to the rescue of the country, scholars have found that the average minuteman was, economically speaking, below average. The average American was middle-class. According to Robert Gross's study of the Concord militia, the average minuteman, after 1778, was poor, landless, out of work, and out of hope. If Gross is right, the minuteman's decision to volunteer did not come at the expense of his career. If anything, the war provided men with opportunities for social advancement they otherwise wouldn't have had.

Many a minuteman wasn't really a volunteer anyway; many were paid to fight. When the yeoman farmer didn't want to heed the call of the militia, he frequently hired a substitute to do his fighting for him.[4]

The idea that Americans don't need to prepare for war because in a pinch they can always rely on the citizen militia stems from another misconception involving the minuteman. It is based on the belief, as a military man once lamented, that Lexington and Concord proved that "the old squirrel rifle from the mantelpiece will repulse any foe." In truth, Lexington and Concord proved, if anything, just how unreliable the minuteman was without thorough training.[5]

While every boy and girl is taught to think of the minuteman as a great shot, evidence suggests he wasn't much of a sharpshooter after all—at least not at Lexington and Concord. Stewart Holbrook estimates that "not one American in ten hit a redcoat that seething day."* More redcoats than Americans were killed and wounded in the battles, but that was only because the Americans outnumbered the British by about two to one. Concludes Holbrook: "That [the Americans] wreaked as much destruction as they did was because there were so many of them shooting."[6]

---

*The minuteman's inability to shoot straight is easily explained. Farmers had experience shooting buckshot, but they needed greater accuracy to shoot bullets. Even if the farmers had wanted to practice shooting bullets, they couldn't. Gunpowder was in scarce supply.

Further confusion surrounds the actual behavior of the minuteman at Lexington when they came under fire. Some authors say they "stood their ground." Others insist they "confronted" the redcoats. The fact is, according to the minutemen's own leader, Captain John Parker, they scattered—as they were told to. "Upon [the redcoats'] sudden approach," recalled Parker in a deposition given after the incident, "I immediately ordered our Militia to disperse and not to fire."

Parker did not say whether at the time he had remarked, as we've been taught to believe, "Don't fire unless fired upon, but if they mean to have a war, let it begin here." Chances are he did not. As with many other famous quotes, this one has a dubious pedigree. It did not surface until 1858. The person who brought it to the attention of the world was Parker's grandson.[7]

In contrast with the heroic image of the minuteman is the sad picture of the original army recruit. While the minuteman could just spring to arms successfully overnight, the average soldier had to work hard just to achieve mediocrity. As the story goes, he finally becomes a great soldier, but it takes nothing less than the intervention of a stern Prussian taskmaster, the legendary Baron Friedrich von Steuben, to make him one. The truth is the minuteman probably was not as good as people think, and the army recruit not as bad.

Misconceptions abound not only about the people who fought the war but about the kind of war they fought. Myth to the contrary, the Revolution was mainly fought—by both sides—in the classic European style. Guerrilla warfare was rare. As one historian indicates, the American Revolution was not England's Vietnam— at least not as far as military tactics go—and George Washington was not Ho Chi Minh—at least to the extent that Ho was a guerrilla chieftain. In the end the Americans won not because they had amassed a great guerrilla army but because they had learned how to use a regular army to beat a regular army. Historian Don Higginbotham says the Americans deliberately rejected the option of a guerrilla war because they feared its consequences: "A guerrilla war that might achieve independence but wreck the institutions of society in the process would be a hollow victory; Americans had no wish to win the war and lose the peace." He points out that it's not certain the Americans would, in any case, have won such a war. The British had just as much experience fighting guerrilla wars as the Americans. Both had had the experience, after all, of fighting Indians.[8]

Equally as surprising as the myths about the conduct of the Revolutionary War are the myths about its leaders, many of whom are overestimated. Everyone remembers John Paul Jones's contribution on the high seas and that he supposedly remarked, "I've just begun to fight"; almost no one recalls that after the Revolution John Paul Jones, defender of liberty, became a well-paid mercenary in the service of the great Russian despot Catherine the Great. Also forgotten are that Alexander Hamilton submitted to blackmail after he had seduced an associate's wife;* that Robert Morris, the financier of the Revolution, used his public position to enrich his private firm and was accused of war profiteering; that Silas Deane, one of the negotiators of the Franco-American Treaty of Alliance, used inside diplomatic information to make himself rich; and that Paul Revere was convicted of "lack of proper spirit" (in effect, cowardice) for his part as chief artillery officer in the failed Penobscot expedition, the worst naval disaster of the Revolution.[9]

Revere was for the most part a hero, but his role in warning of approaching redcoats has been exaggerated. Thanks to Longfellow, everyone thinks Revere rode alone through the woods when the British started in on Lexington and Concord. Actually two others—William Dawes and Samuel Prescott—also made the trip. Revere did not even make it to Concord. After warning Lexington, he ran into a British patrol and was captured.[10]

Ethan Allen, of Green Mountain Boy fame, is probably the most overrated revolutionary hero; he may even qualify as another Benedict Arnold. Allen is commonly thought to have accomplished wonderful things for his country, not least of which was

---

* After the blackmail was paid, Hamilton was accused of conspiring with the woman's husband in improper speculative schemes. This wasn't true, but to save himself from the charge that he had violated his public trust, Hamilton had to reveal his private vice. "The charge against me," he explained, "is a connection with one James Reynolds for purposes of improper pecuniary speculation. My real crime is an amorous connection with his wife." (See Harold Syrett, ed., *The Papers of Alexander Hamilton* [1974], vol. XXI, pp. 243–44.)

the storming of Fort Ticonderoga in a sensational raid of derring-do. But if Henry Steele Commager and Samuel Eliot Morison are to be believed—and few historians are more respected than they— Allen deserves to go down in history as one of its great scoundrels. Commager and Morison report that in the middle of the war, unbeknown to his contemporaries, Allen opened secret negotiations with the enemy, apparently to try to secure royal recognition of more than a quarter million acres of disputed Vermont land his family claimed. At one point he even promised to take Vermont out of the war in return for certain land concessions. The British wouldn't go along, however, and the deal fell through.

Some Allen supporters have suggested he was only trying to put pressure on Congress to guarantee Vermont statehood. Maybe, but just communicating with the British during the war was considered a crime; Allen himself had a hand in sending to the gallows a man who had committed this very offense. Had *his* dealings with the British been discovered, Allen might have faced a similar end.[11]

A curious legend about Benedict Arnold, by the way, is that when he was about to die, he put on his old American uniform. One author even has Arnold saying, "Let me die in my American uniform in which I fought my battles. God forgive me for ever putting on any other."

Nice story—if it were true, but it isn't. All the evidence suggests it not only didn't happen but couldn't have happened. After he died, his wife wrote that Arnold was delirious his last three days and was entirely unable to swallow or speak.[12]

The War of 1812 is neither celebrated nor scorned. It's simply ignored. Its chief significance, in the popular understanding, is that it occasioned the burning of Washington, D.C. This is remembered as a great and dastardly deed and for some time afterward constituted a major black mark against the British. What is usually left unsaid is that the British burned our capital only after Americans had burned one of their parliaments.

The American attack occurred near Lake Ontario, at York,

the capital of Upper Canada, at the end of April 1813. Washington was set afire in the summer of 1814.

To be fair about it, the Americans acted without orders, and their superiors didn't even know what was happening until after the attack. In contrast, the British officers not only were aware of the burning of Washington but ordered it. Still, to say the British were therefore more culpable than the Americans is simply the American viewpoint. The British see things differently.[13]

Another controversy between the British and the Americans is the question of the circumstances surrounding Thomas Macdonough's victory on Lake Champlain. Everyone agrees Macdonough, an American, won, but they don't agree about which side had the superior fleet. American historians frequently claim that Macdonough was outgunned and outmanned. British historians say just the opposite: that the American forces were superior (it being better to be defeated by a larger force than by a smaller one).

The fact is both sides were about even. Each had a frigate and a brig and almost the same number of gunboats (twelve for the British, ten for the Americans). In addition, the British had two sloops; the Americans, a sloop and a schooner. The British had more long guns, but the Americans had a far greater number of short cannons. What all this meant was that the Americans could fire more pounds of ammunition, but the British could fire what they had from farther away.[14]

Unlike the War of 1812, the war for Texas independence is the focus of a number of enduring myths, most having to do with the brave stand taken at the Alamo in 1836 by the likes of William Travis, Jim Bowie, and Davy Crockett—themselves the subject of myth.

Americans living in the Southwest know the basic story better than others, but everybody knows the essential fact that the defenders of the Alamo fought to the last man. Americans usually don't like celebrating losses, but this defeat was different because it ended on a sublime note. The moral: If you have to lose, this is the way to do it.

How did the last defenders actually die? How did Davy die? Not, as it turns out, in the midst of battle. According to historian Dan Kilgore, overwhelming evidence indicates that Crockett and several Texans were captured by General Antonia López de Santa Anna and then executed; they did not die fighting to the end. If Mexican General Manuel Fernández Castrillón had had his way, they would have been spared. Santa Anna overruled Castrillón and had them killed.

The question is why anyone ever started the myth that the defenders had fought to the last man anyway. The real story of the Alamo is good enough as is. The defenders had shown remarkable courage in fighting at all rather than surrendering right from the first; the 182 Americans holed up in the old church were vastly outnumbered by more than 6,000 Mexican troops. Even considering the low quality of the average Mexican recruit in those days, the odds of victory were negligible. Some have suggested the Americans remained only because they expected to be rescued by reinforcements any day, but that doesn't diminish the bravery of the men who stayed rather than run.

Travis is remembered in a vague way mainly for the line he allegedly drew in the dirt at the outset of the fight; only those willing to fight for Texas independence, he supposedly said, should cross it. Well, he may have said such a thing, but it's doubtful. The anecdote apparently relies on an account published nearly forty years later by a man who got the story from his parents, who in turn claimed to have gotten it from one Moses Rose, who hadn't crossed the line and had fled.

It's a good thing Travis isn't remembered for much else because the rest of his story is not particularly heroic. Before going to Texas, he lived in Alabama, where he killed a man who made advances on his wife. A short time later he left his wife and son to move to Texas at a time when she was pregnant. When he arrived in Texas, he lied about his family, swearing under oath in one place that he was a widower and in another that he was a simple bachelor.[15]

*   *   *

The Mexican-American War, which was precipitated by the war for Texas independence, is not the subject of any major myths. It is barely even recalled, probably for the better. A war for pure territory, as this war was, is not the kind of war Americans care to celebrate or mythologize, nor should they.

The Civil War has been both celebrated and mythologized. The only trouble is that no two historians seem to agree on what is truth and what is fiction. They agree in general that slavery was a fundamental cause of the war, but that's about all. Was the conflict "irrepressible"? Were "natural causes" to blame? Were the abolitionists at fault? Don't ask historians. They don't agree. All this proves, if anyone needs such evidence, is that one person's truth is another person's myth. This is, of course, true about most historical arguments, but seemingly truer about the Civil War than about many others. "There must be more historians of the Civil War than there were generals fighting in it," historian David Donald has observed. "[And] of the two groups, the historians are the more belligerent."[16]

But if there is no consensus on what caused the conflict, people have agreed on what didn't cause it. No respectable person today blames the war on a slaveholders' conspiracy as contemporaries did. Neither does anyone attribute the war to fanatical Republican politicians, as once was the fashion. Except for historian E. B. Smith, no one recently has seriously argued that the war was caused by a blundering generation of pompous, self-interested, fanatical politicians.

One still does hear the self-flagellating idea that slavery was harsher in the United States than anywhere else in the modern Western world and that therefore, only here was war required to root it out. The classic statement is made by one Frank Tannenbaum in an influential little book called *Slave and Citizen*, published in 1946. As Tannenbaum puts it, slavery in Latin America was milder than in the United States, and manumission (the release of slaves), easier. "The principle of manumission," writes Tannenbaum, "provided Latin American slavery a means of change.

The denial of manumission [in the United States] encrusted the social structure in the Southern states and left no escape except by revolution, which in this case took the form of a civil war."

Would it were so, for the American Civil War would then be easy to explain. It isn't. Thorough investigation has revealed that while the Civil War was exceptionally violent, the abolition of slavery in Latin America occasioned serious disruption as well. David Brion Davis, who has studied slavery more closely probably than any other living person, has discovered that the abolition of slavery in Brazil and the Caribbean closely followed the pattern of the United States. In Brazil, says Davis, "there was a radical abolition movement, an underground railroad, and sectional cleavage," just as in North America. And abolition brought down government leaders; in the case of Brazil, it ended the monarchy. In the Caribbean British planters threatened secession when the crown ordered the slaves freed; the planters relented only after they realized it would be suicidal to resist in the face of overwhelming British military superiority.

Only in the United States did abolitionism lead to civil war, but that may have been for any number of reasons. One scholar has even suggested that federalism may have been to blame.[17]

Other Civil War myths concern the famous Bixby letter, the Andersonville prison, and Jefferson Davis's "dress." Although the celebrated letter to Mrs. Bixby sounds like Lincoln, scholars say there's no proof he wrote it, read it, or even signed it. Like most of the letters he sent to strangers, this one, addressed "to the mother of five sons who have died gloriously on the field of battle," may have been written by one of his secretaries. Lincoln's secretary John Hay, indeed, claimed he had written the letter, though it's unclear whether he meant he had composed it or just penned it.[*]

Whoever wrote it, it was a beautiful letter—but it was also a beautiful hoax. According to War Department statistics, only two Bixby sons were killed, while one deserted, one was honorably

---

[*] The letter reads, in part: "I feel how weak and fruitless must be any word of mine which should attempt to beguile you from the grief of a loss so overwhelming. But I cannot refrain from tendering to you the consolation that may be found in the thanks of the Republic they died to save."

discharged, and one was captured and became a Confederate.[18]

As for Andersonville, it was a vile prison. It may have been the worst prison. But it wasn't the only prison where captured soldiers died cruel and needless deaths. POWs died in northern prisons, too. In fact, death rates in POW camps in the North and South were comparable. Of the 195,000 Union soldiers imprisoned in the South, 15.5 percent died in prison; of the 215,000 Confederates imprisoned in the North, 12 percent died in prison.

More POWs died in Andersonville than in any other prison— more than twelve thousand in all, more than a hundred a day. But it's not as if the South had deliberately planned things that way. The Confederates just couldn't afford to do better. While rations were meager, records show that the prisoners received the same amount of rations as the Confederates who guarded them.[19]

As for Jefferson Davis, for all his humiliations, the Confederate president did not disguise himself in his wife's clothing to try to avoid capture. When he was arrested, he was wearing regular clothes, including a man's hat. All the pictures showing him dressed like a woman, all the cartoons—all are wrong. "I was in the party that captured Davis," Captain James H. Parker wrote later, "and saw the whole transaction from its beginning. I now say, and hope that you will publish it, that Jefferson Davis did not have on, at the time he was taken, any garments such as are worn by women."

No one knows how the rumor got started. But we know how it spread: by military officials. They got it from hearsay. Reporters got it from them.[20]

By almost any standard, the Spanish-American War ranks as a minor conflict, but it's the source of major confusion. Not even the famous Rough Riders are accurately remembered. Everybody thinks the Rough Riders charged around on horses, whereas they actually fought on foot because their horses had mistakenly been left behind in Florida. The impression that the Rough Riders formed a major part of the land forces is also common but untrue; they numbered just a few hundred men out of an army of more than sixteen thousand. Teddy Roosevelt is remembered for charging up

San Juan Hill, though he probably went up nearby Kettle Hill. He himself is responsible for the confusion. Although originally he spoke of Kettle Hill, years later he talked about San Juan Hill. Finally, textbook writers almost always say that the war marked America's entrance onto the world stage, but in truth it had been there long before. Thomas A. Bailey was one of those writers, but he later recanted, remarking: "The flash of Dewey's guns merely spotlighted a maturation that had long since taken place. The irony is that we finally won belated acceptance into the great power 'club' by thrashing a second-rate power in two naval engagements that cost us only one life."[21]

Admiral George Dewey is thought to have made a reputation for himself in the war, and he did that; but it didn't last. Two years later it was smashed like the Spanish fleet. Once again Dewey did the smashing. Americans had liked Dewey and talked about running the war hero for President in 1900. But when he announced that he was interested in the job, he blundered badly. He told reporters that he had worried at first he wasn't well enough qualified, but that then he had looked into the office a bit and discovered he could do the job all right despite his own modest abilities. He said that "the office of the president is not such a very difficult one to fill," and that was the last anyone heard of Admiral Dewey. After his remarks no one wanted to run him for President—or anything.[22]

World War I is not now so much a source of myth as it once was. No one today seriously believes, as contemporaries did, the claim of Allied propaganda that the Germans were guilty of unprecedented murder and mayhem of civilians. As is now well known, many of the atrocities attributed to the Germans were simply made up; besides, both sides committed horrible acts. What's more, a lot of people in the 1930's believed Wall Street had pushed America into the Great War to save bankers' loans, but by the 1940's almost no one responsible held this view. It didn't make much sense. The billions in loans made to the Allies were considered safe; bankers thought the Allies were winning and would repay the

Legends, Lies, and Cherished Myths

money after victory. Besides, it's unlikely the Congress would ever have agreed to send American boys off to certain death in a foreign land just to salvage the fortunes of a few financiers.

Yet myths remain, as befits a war about which there was so much confusion that Americans weren't even sure when it ended. Everyone now knows this war to end all wars ended at the eleventh hour of the eleventh day of the eleventh month in 1918. Indeed, on that day Americans celebrated the war's end, but not vigorously. The country had already gone through one celebration—four days earlier—when a United Press dispatch falsely reported the war was over. It wasn't; soldiers were still dying in battle. However, the country didn't know that until the next day, when the wire service finally put out a correction.[23]

The commonest erroneous beliefs about World War I are that the sinking of the *Lusitania* touched off American intervention, that submarine warfare was invented by the Germans, and that Germany was bankrupted by the Versailles Treaty.

While the sinking of the *Lusitania* heightened anti-German feeling, it did not precipitate American intervention, which didn't occur for another two years. (The *Lusitania* was sunk in 1915.) When the ship was struck, 128 Americans died, but the *Lusitania* wasn't an American ship; it was British. The ship wasn't struck without warning; before it sailed, the Germans issued a warning that it would be targeted by submarines. As if all this weren't enough, the *Lusitania* was carrying small arms and ammunition; it wasn't exactly an unarmed passenger ship, as propagandists asserted.[24]

Another popular error—that the Germans invented submarine warfare—is less egregious. The Germans did perfect warfare by submarine; they just didn't invent it. Americans did. During the Revolution George Washington used a primitive one-man submarine to try to blow up the British *Eagle*, a sixty-four-gun warship tied up in New York Harbor. The effort failed, however, because the submarine operator couldn't attach the bomb to the British ship's frame. While Washington remained a submarine enthusiast, Congress was not enthralled and refused to appropriate any money for future operations. In the Civil War the Confederates resorted to submarine warfare to try to break the North's blockade. This effort was more successful than Washington's, but not by much. The Confederates managed to sink one ship and damage another, but the two submarines involved in the attacks were destroyed in the process.[25]

The belief that Germany was bankrupted by the Versailles Treaty was advanced by the foremost economist of the century John Maynard Keynes and is frequently considered the chief cause of Adolf Hitler's rise to power. Actually, Germany was responsible for Germany's economic troubles; the demand for war reparations made at Versailles had little to do with the matter. The First World War cost Germany about $100 billion; war reparations only came to about $32 billion. Undoubtedly the reparations demanded in the Versailles Treaty strained the German economy, but it was probably already ruined by war. As a comparison, consider this: Germany spent almost as much on World War I as the United States, forty years later, spent on Vietnam. (America spent about $120 billion.) Put another way, German outlays during the war equaled the entire United States budget in 1965.

That Germany was bankrupt after the war, for whatever reason, is taken for granted by almost everyone, but it may not be true. Economist John Kenneth Galbraith has suggested that the German economy was adequate to support the country's population after the war. He has even argued that the Germans could have met reparations demands if they had so desired by accepting a lower standard of living. This would have been an unpleasant development, says Galbraith, but not an impossible one.

It may be that Galbraith is being iconoclastic just to be so. In that case the conventional wisdom may be true. The fact is no one can ever know for sure. To prove that Germany could have afforded to pay war reparations, one would have to do one of those computer studies that show how history might have happened. Such studies are notoriously unreliable. One is reminded of the study a few years ago that suggested America would have been better off building canals than railroads. It was done by the same fellow who subsequently reported that computer analyses show that slavery wasn't very harsh. He may be right in both instances, but he didn't have to tote that barge or lift that bale.[26]

An interesting footnote to the stories about the First World War and its aftermath touches on a myth involving the United States and Russia. It is widely believed that Americans and Russians have never clashed in battle, but they did fight on two occasions, with casualties on both sides. In 1918 and 1919 five thousand American troops were sent to northern Russia, and nine thousand to Siberia. Ostensibly American troops went to Russia as part of the effort to defeat Germany: Troops in the north were to stiffen local opposition to the Germans; troops in Siberia were to help keep open the Trans-Siberian Railroad, which was being used to rescue cornered Czech troops. American soldiers were under orders not to take sides in the Russian Revolution, then in full swing. But inevitably they did. Gradually drawn into the internal conflict, Americans ended up fighting on the side of the counter-revolutionaries against the Bolsheviks. In the campaign in northern Russia there were five hundred American casualties; in the Siberian operation, thirty-six Americans died.[27]

Unlike World War I, World War II is still very much a source of outlandish myths, most having to do with Pearl Harbor. One hears from time to time, for instance, the old charge that Franklin Roosevelt deliberately exposed the fleet in Hawaii to provoke a Japanese attack. It just isn't so. Warnings had gone out to the fleet commanders to be prepared for war prior to the attack, but the commanders never anticipated Japan would strike Pearl Harbor. The military reasoned that before Japan targeted American possessions, it would first exercise its muscle in its own backyard, taking over such likely marks as Thailand, British Malaya, or the Dutch East Indies.

Just prior to the attack there had been several events that might have alarmed an alert commander. A couple of hours before the attack a Japanese submarine had been spotted and destroyed. Less than an hour before the attack radar picked up signs of approaching aircraft. But no one thought the appearance of either the submarine or the planes was significant.*

There had been one hint that the Japanese might assault Pearl Harbor. Eleven months before the "day of infamy" the American ambassador to Japan had picked up a rumor that the Japanese planned a surprise attack on Pearl Harbor. It was unfortunately only one of many wild rumors then circulating and didn't attract much attention. Rumors contradicted each other; no one knew which rumors to take seriously.[28]

Few Americans believe the false stories about Pearl Harbor, but other major myths about World War II are widespread and worth mentioning. These include myths about German war preparations, Hitler, Jews, and the atomic bomb.

Nazi propaganda is responsible for the widely held conviction that Germany (in historian A.J.P. Taylor's phrase) "had armed day and night from the moment Hitler came to power." Among other things, Americans believe that in the prewar days Hitler put the German economy on a wartime footing, that German factories operated at 100 percent capacity, that Germany had an advantage over the Allies because of its war preparations, and that the Nazis turned the German economy into a ruthless, efficient machine.

All this is (Taylor again) "pure myth." The United States government, after an exhaustive postwar investigation, came to the conclusion that through most of the war years the German economy was run by incompetent Nazis, that war preparations were nil. Right until the end of the war the economy was still geared to civilian needs. The Germans seemed almost bent on wasting valuable resources. In 1943 they imported fifty thousand Ukranian women to do household chores. As late as 1944 they were still employing servants in large numbers—as many as 1.3 million. Even at the end of the war German war factories mainly operated only in daytime; few bothered with nighttime shifts.

The famous blitzkrieg attacks, so feared in the West, were dictated by German economic conditions. The German economy

*The planes were thought to be American. However, the American planes were expected from the east, while the blips on the radar screen indicated a flight path from the north. No one realized that.

couldn't support sustained warfare, so the military had to resort to lightning-quick strikes to achieve prompt victories. The Germans took advantage of the intervening lulls to restore depleted stocks in time for the next attack. This was for a time a successful strategy, and that was fortunate for the Nazis; they couldn't fight and win any other way. They couldn't afford to.*

The Allies were far better prepared for war. In 1941 Britain, with 70 percent of the national income of Germany, outproduced the Nazis in virtually every armaments category except torpedoes and small arms. It produced twice as many aircraft as Germany, a thousand more tanks, five thousand more big guns. If any people deserves to be remembered as efficient and productive, it is not the Germans but the British.[29]

As misleading as the belief in German war preparedness is the related conviction that Hitler nefariously plotted in advance to make war on all Europe in order to take over the world. Indeed, it is sometimes suggested he plotted Germany's conquest of the world years earlier from inside the walls of prison while he was mulling over the German humiliation at Versailles. There is no evidence at all that this is true. As Taylor reported in 1960, Hitler seems to have drifted into world war one small victory at a time and himself seemed surprised the early triumphs came so easily. People find this hard to fathom, however, and believe it somehow excuses Hitler's behavior. As Taylor wrote, "Somehow people regard planning war as more wicked than waging a successful war unplanned." That, of course, is nonsense.[30]

Whether Hitler planned the war or not, everyone knows that at the 1936 Olympics he snubbed Jesse Owens. As the story goes,

---

* Fascists may be consoled by the fact that at least Benito Mussolini made the trains run on time. Or did he? To quote Bergen Evans, "[T]he trains did *not* run on time! [I] was employed as a courier by the Franco-Belgique Tours Company in the summer of 1930, Mussolini's heyday, when a fascist guard rode on every train, and [I am] willing to make an affidavit to the effect that *most* Italian trains on which [I] traveled were not on schedule—or near it. There must be thousands who can support this attestation. It's a trifle, but it's worth nailing down."

Evans notes that the Nazis weren't very efficient either. "German invasion maps of England, when captured," he writes, "turned out to be common Ordnance Survey maps, purchasable at any stationer's for a few pence, and twenty years out of date, lacking new highways, bridges, bypaths, and vital targets. A map of Oxford, for instance, marks the University as a single building in New College Lane." (See Bergen Evans's *The Spoor of Spooks* [1954], p. 77n.)

after Owens won one gold medal, Hitler, incensed, stormed out of Olympic Stadium so he wouldn't have to congratulate Owens on his victory.

Such a performance would have been perfectly in character, but it didn't happen. William J. Baker, Owens's biographer, says the newspapers made up the whole story. Owens himself originally insisted it wasn't true, but eventually he began saying it was, apparently out of sheer boredom with the issue.

The facts are simple. Hitler did not congratulate Owens, but that day he didn't congratulate anybody else either, not even the German winners. As a matter of fact, Hitler didn't congratulate anyone after the first day of the competition. That first day he had shaken hands with all the German victors, but that had gotten him in trouble with the members of the Olympic Committee. They told him that to maintain Olympic neutrality, he would have to congratulate everyone or no one. Hitler chose to honor no one.

Hitler did snub a black American athlete, but it was Cornelius Johnson, not Jesse Owens. It happened the first day of the meet. Just before Johnson was to be decorated, Hitler left the stadium. A Nazi spokesman explained that Hitler's exit had been prescheduled, but no one believes that.

Several other misconceptions about the 1936 Olympics are prevalent. Not only was Owens not rebuffed by Hitler, Owens wasn't shunned by the German audience at the Berlin stadium either. Baker reports that Owens so captured the imagination of the crowd it gave him several ear-shattering ovations.

Owens had been prepared for a hostile reception; a coach had warned him in advance not to be upset by anything that might happen in the stands. "Ignore the insults," Owens was told, "and you'll be all right." Later Owens recalled that he had gotten the greatest ovations of his career at Berlin.

Another popular belief is that the games marked a humiliating moment for the Nazis because a few blacks walked away with a fistful of medals while Hitler had predicted the Teutonic lads would be the big winners, proof of the superman abilities of the white race. In reality, the competition was anything but a German

Legends, Lies, and Cherished Myths

humiliation. It is forgotten that Germany managed to pick up more medals than all the other countries combined. Hitler was pleased with the outcome.[31]

No aspect of Hitler's Germany has possibly received more attention than the treatment of the Jews, but myths remain. When at the end of the war Edward R. Murrow conducted a well-publicized radio tour of the Nazi death camps, it seemed everybody finally became convinced of their existence. The wonder is that it took so long. Evidence that Jews were being slaughtered by the millions had been abundant and overwhelming for years.

The news did not just trickle out in the waning hours of the Nazi empire. The first slaughter took place in 1941, when about half a million Jews were killed by mobile Nazi murder units. In July word of the deaths reached the American Jewish press and was reported in New York City's Yiddish dailies. In October 1941 *The New York Times* carried an article on the machine-gunning of thousands of Jews in Poland and the Ukraine. In the summer of 1942 a German industrialist, at risk to his life, leaked word to the Allies of Hitler's systematic plan to exterminate the Jews. In the months following, mass meetings were held in New York and several other cities to protest the Nazi's "Final Solution." One magazine published an article unequivocally entitled "Murder of a People."

The news of the Holocaust did not, however, make big news during the war. A historian who has made an exceptionally detailed study of the matter says that "the mass media treated the systematic murder of millions of Jews as though it were minor news." Even *The New York Times* routinely published stories on the Holocaust deep on the inside pages. It was on page twelve, in four short column inches, that the *Times* reported the extermination of four hundred thousand Hungarian Jews in 1944.

The mistaken public impression that news of the Holocaust did not come until after the war is thus easily explained: It wasn't until after the war that the news made the front pages. Less understandable is why that was so. Perhaps genocide on such a scale was so unprecedented that journalists couldn't quite believe it was true. Putting the story on the back pages gave it less credence. Too, they may have remembered the stories of German atrocities in World War I that turned out, after the war, to have been nothing more than war propaganda. No one likes to be taken in twice.

The prevailing belief that the American people would have tried to do something to stop the Holocaust and would have tried to save the Jews if the situation had been understood is possible but doubtful. (Elie Wiesel: "Was the free world aware of what was going on? Surely not; otherwise it would have done something to prevent such a massacre.")

Government leaders did in fact know—and did nothing. They told Jewish groups that pressed for action that the only way to save the Jews was to win the war and that they were doing that as quickly as possibly. When FDR was asked to bomb the death camp at Auschwitz, the military said it couldn't spare the planes to do the job, even though bombers were hitting targets just fifty miles away. David Wyman, the leading expert on the American response to the Holocaust, says the government could have saved the lives of hundreds of thousands of Jews without harming the war effort if it really wanted to, but it didn't want to. American leaders, particularly in the State Department, says Wyman, did not want to face the possibility that the Jews, if rescued, could end up in the United States. He says American Jewish leaders themselves didn't vigorously pursue plans to rescue the Jews because they were preoccupied with dreams of building a Jewish homeland in Palestine.[32]

The chief confusion about the atomic bomb has to do with the decision to drop it on Japan. Paul Johnson, like many popular historians, contends it was a necessity, disagreeable as it may have been, because it undoubtedly saved lives. The claim is that but for the bomb, the United States would have had to invade the Japanese Islands and at frightening cost; the military estimated at the time such an effort might cause up to a million American casualties and perhaps as many as ten to twenty million Japanese deaths.

(The bombs at Hiroshima and Nagasaki killed fewer than half a million people all told.) Skeptics are assured the Japanese intended to fight to the last man, as indicated in a secret document approved by the Japanese Supreme Council on June 6, 1945, which revealed the government's intention to "prosecute the war to the bitter end." Further, it's said that Japan had made plans to dispatch ten thousand so-called suicide planes and, in a desperation move, was prepared to field a civilian militia of thirty million.

Yet doubt remains, not least because the United States government itself concluded after the war we hadn't needed to drop the A-bombs. In 1946 the United States Strategic Bombing Survey, after an exhaustive study, found that the Japanese were about to surrender when the bombs hit. "Based on detailed investigation of all the facts," says the survey, "and supported by the testimony of the surviving Japanese leaders involved, it is the Survey's opinion that certainly prior to 31 December 1945, and in all probability prior to 1 November 1945, Japan would have surrendered even if the atomic bombs had not been dropped, even if Russia had not entered the war, and even if no invasion had been planned or contemplated." On June 20, 1945, the emperor and leading members of the Supreme War Direction Council had secretly decided to end the war. John Kenneth Galbraith, a member of the survey team, says that nothing more insurmountable than the "usual bureaucratic lags" kept the Japanese from suing for peace immediately.[33]

The often-repeated allegation that the decision to drop the atomic bomb was horrid in light of the known effects of radiation is misinformed. *No one knew anyone would die of radiation.* Not even those who created the bomb in the first place knew that. When the Japanese began reporting that victims were dying of radiation poisoning, scientists insisted the Japanese must be lying. The scientists had told the United States press that the radioactive effects of the bomb would be minor. They refused to believe they were wrong. One colonel reacted angrily to a Tokyo commentator's lament that the people of Hiroshima were "doomed to die of radioactivity." Said the colonel: "That's kind of crazy. I would say this: I think it's good propaganda. The thing is these people got good and burned—good thermal burns."

Only slowly did scientists become convinced of the accuracy of the initial reports. Years later one of the leading experts in the Manhattan Project, Dr. Norman Ramsey, recalled in an oral memoir how surprised everyone was by what happened. "The people who made the decision to drop the bomb made it on the assumption that all casualties would be standard explosion casualties. . . . The region over which there would have been radiation injury was to be a much smaller one than the region of so-called 100% blast kill. . . . Any person with radiation damage would have been killed with a brick first." As one historian concluded, "The men who made the Bomb did not know what it was."[34]

Two or three other myths that came out of the war, less important but well known, continue to cause trouble and are worth refuting. That bombers won the war in Europe is the theme of countless Hollywood movies and is the conceit of the U.S. Air Force, but it is without foundation. While tactical air strikes helped immeasurably in the war, strategic bombing runs helped little, if at all. Galbraith says the bombing campaign was probably the "greatest miscalculation of the war."

Naturally, not everyone agrees with Galbraith, and that of course, is how he likes it. But he has the impressive support, again, of the United States Strategic Bombing Survey, of which he was a leading member.

Two of the survey's findings seem especially convincing. First, the survey discovered that German economic production actually increased after the bombing campaign got fully under way. The common delusion that production decreased—it just had to—is belied by the statistics. The monthly production of panzers, for instance, steadily rose during the war, from 136 in 1940, to 136 in 1941, to 516 in 1942, to 1,005 in 1943. In the final two years, despite massive bombings, the Germans produced some 1,500 panzers a month.

Second, the survey found, much to the surprise of its own members, that even factories directly hit by bombs weren't put out of action, at least not for very long. The Germans, it seems, learned they could quickly rescue the machinery in bombed-out factories and simply set up shop nearby.

As if all this weren't discouraging enough, Galbraith insists the bombing campaign may have even helped the Germans *increase* production. By bombing German cities, the air force helped destroy the urban service economy; this in turn freed waiters and others to man the country's labor-short factories, located on the outskirts of cities. Ironically, the American air force was helping the German generals achieve what they couldn't on their own: a war-based economy. That, if Galbraith is correct, may explain, partly anyway, how the Germans were able to produce more panzers at the end of the war than at the start.[35]

The self-sacrificing spirit of Americans during the war, frequently noted, is exaggerated. Rationing was often undermined by extensive black-market dealing, which was observed at the time. Soldiers complained the folks back home didn't take the war seriously enough. Americans at home agreed. In 1945 Dr. George Gallup found that six in ten Americans believed they hadn't made significant sacrifices during the war. Some of those who claimed they had seemed not to understand the meaning of the word "sacrifice." A waitress in Dayton, Ohio, complained, "All my boy friends have gone overseas; so I can't get married." A stenographer in Detroit grumbled, "I've had to get along without nylons."[36]

Myths about Vietnam are less prevalent now than earlier, but one in particular has hung on.[37] Americans still seem to believe the country's leaders slipped into war in ignorance of what they were getting into. This isn't true. Both Kennedy and Johnson had been warned repeatedly that the effort to save South Vietnam from communism could cost the United States dearly and might very well result in failure. When Kennedy authorized the dispatch of seven thousand troops to Vietnam, he was told by General Maxwell Taylor that "there is no limit to our possible commitment." Kennedy himself seemed to recognize the danger. As he told Arthur Schlesinger, Jr., "The troops will march in; the bands will play; the crowds will cheer; and in four days everyone will have forgotten. Then we will be told to send in more troops. It's like taking a drink. The effect wears off, and you have to take another."

Americans who still insist Kennedy and Johnson really didn't understand the sacrifice the war would require may be interested in the remarkable warning General Charles de Gaulle issued in May 1961. In a private conversation with Kennedy the French president warned that a land war in Asia could not be won.

You will find that intervention in this area will be an endless entanglement. Once a nation has been aroused, no foreign power, however strong, can impose its will upon it. You will discover this for yourselves. For even if you find local leaders who in their own interests are prepared to obey you, the people will not agree to it, and indeed do not want it. The ideology which you invoke will make no difference. Indeed, in the eyes of the masses, it will become identified with your will to power. That is why the more you become involved out there against the Communists, the more the Communists will appear as the champions of national independence, and the more support they will receive, if only from despair. We French have had experience of it. You Americans want to take our place. I predict you will sink step by step into a bottomless military and political quagmire, however much you spend in men and money.

Claims that the American military misled American leaders into believing war could easily be won are widespread but unfounded. Early in the war Johnson was told by his own Chairman of the Joint Chiefs of Staff, General Earl Wheeler, that victory in Vietnam would take seven hundred thousand to a million soldiers and extend over seven years. As Paul Johnson has remarked, "[President] Johnson went into the war with his eyes open."[38]

Immigrants

Immigrants are sentimental favorites in American lore, but much of the sentiment often is condescending and inaccurate. Even the famous poem by Emma Lazarus on the Statue of Liberty, which was written in connection with the immigration of the Irish Catholics and Jews in the nineteenth century, is riddled with errors. The contention that the immigrants who came over by boat were tired, for instance, belies the fact that they had to possess an awful lot of energy just to make the trip. As U.S. Senator Daniel Patrick Moynihan has observed, "So far as I can remember, [my Irish immigrant grandfather] never once mentioned being tired."

As for the business about "your poor,/Your huddled masses yearning to breathe free," there's the inconvenient fact that the world into which they arrived—New York City—was a cesspool of intrigue and poverty and corruption. "Put plain," says Moynihan, "the immigrants of the second half of the nineteenth century came from societies more civilized than ours." We didn't have pogroms, of course; but we did have lynchings, and at the turn of the century lynchings were common. On average there was a lynching a day.

As for the claim about the "wretched refuse of your teeming shore," there's reason to ask, as Moynihan has, What wretched refuse? As he has said, "The 20 million-odd immigrants who arrived between 1870 and 1910 were not the wretched refuse of anybody's shores. They were an extraordinary, enterprising, and self-sufficient folk who knew exactly what they were doing, and doing it quite on their own, thank you very much." In fact, they weren't any more wretched than any other immigrant groups, including the Pilgrims. They deserve to be remembered not as a teeming mass, unkempt, uneducated, and uncouth but as the energetic bunch of enthusiastic go-getters that they actually proved to be.[1]

Whether they were or were not down on their luck when they arrived in America, whether or not they were tired or wretched, it's almost universally believed that once they were here, the immigrants became quick successes. If not they themselves, then certainly their children.

It would be ridiculous to contest the fact that many immigrants did succeed, but success came in such varying degrees, and the term is so loosely defined, as to suggest that the whole subject requires far more discussion than it's usually accorded. Statistics indicate that most immigrants did not exactly become well-to-do. Historian Colin Greer reports that as late as 1950 "more than 80% of New York and New Jersey's working men of Italian and Slavic extraction were employed in unskilled or semi-skilled occupations." More surprising still: "Twenty years later the same phenomenon persisted nationwide. What have now become known as 'white ethnic groups' continued to drop out of school early in large numbers and continue to work in increasingly less available blue collar jobs."

Among immigrant groups, Jews may have come closest to realizing the American dream of success. According to one study, Jews in Boston who arrived in the wave of immigration that began in the 1880's had double the rate of upward mobility as other groups. Jews, though, had an advantage: On average, Jews came

Legends, Lies, and Cherished Myths

to America with far more skills than others. More than half the Jews employed at the turn of the century, for example, had had industrial experience in Europe. Greer says no other immigrants "approached such a percentage." Thus it may be said that while America was indeed a land of opportunity, those who arrived with marketable skills had more opportunity than others. That's not bad, but it somewhat contradicts the national belief in the immigrants' ability to rise as high as their talents would take them. As it turned out, talent wasn't always enough; a good background helped.[2]

It is commonly said that America loves immigrants, but America has actually shown true affection only for a special class of immigrants: immigrants who have been here awhile—a long while. New immigrants almost always have a hard time gaining acceptance here. When the Irish Catholics came over in the early nineteenth century, Protestants, fearful that the "bloody hand of the Pope has stretched itself forth to our destruction," rioted in protest in Philadelphia, setting the Irish part of the city on fire; in the process some thirty houses were burned down, and fourteen people were killed or hurt. When later in the century Southern and Eastern Europeans emigrated to the United States, many old-line Americans reacted as if the country had just been invaded by a horde of criminals. T. B. Aldrich, descendant of an old New England family, lamented:

> O Liberty, white Goddess! is it well
> To leave the gates unguarded?

As hostile as anybody were many Americans who themselves were descended from immigrant families. The word "kike," used to describe the Eastern European Jews, many of whose names ended in *ki*, was coined by New York's long-settled German Jews.[3]

In our own "more civilized" century new immigrants have hardly been treated any better. In the 1910's those from Southern and Eastern Europe even faced the possibility of mass sterilization—or worse. In a popular book endorsed by Theodore Roosevelt, the racist Madison Grant went so far as to suggest that the

state had a moral obligation to put certain immigrant types to death.*
In 1924 the federal government, fed up with the influx of Italian,
Chinese, and Jewish immigrants, decided to limit those who could
come into the country; Italy was limited to four thousand immigrants annually, Russia two thousand, China and Palestine a
hundred apiece. (Great Britain, in contrast, was allowed thirty-
four thousand; Germany, fifty-one thousand) More recently immigrants from Southeast Asia have faced widespread animosity and
discrimination; some, including fishermen along the Texas Gulf
Coast, have even had their livelihoods threatened.[4]

Another belief about the nineteenth-century immigrants—that
they mostly remained here once they got here—has been responsible for a lot of the misinformed criticism of recent Cuban immigrants who have clamored to return home. Americans professed
to be shocked when many of the Cubans who came here in the
Mariel boat lift asked in 1980 to be returned to Cuba. Yet the fact
is that immigrants have always returned home in great numbers.
Historians estimate that of the twenty million immigrants who came
to the United States between 1820 and 1900, about five million
returned to their place of origin.[5]

Of all the questions about immigration, the most studied is
whether America is or is not a melting pot. Even the Congress of
the United States has looked into the matter concluding, in 1972,
that it isn't. Moreover, of all the questions about American immigration, this is the hardest one to answer. All that can be said
for sure is that nothing can be said for sure. Both sides in the
debate are so fully armed with facts they can blow up each other's
arguments with ease without ever winning a decisive victory.

More interesting may be the fact that Americans have thought
of themselves as a melting pot only in this century. Earlier they
generally thought of themselves ethnically as one people. As John
Jay put it in *The Federalist Papers*, this was "one united people, a

---

*In a blurb for Grant's book, *The Passing of the Great Race* (1930), Roosevelt remarked: "The book is a
capital book—in purpose, in vision, in grasp of the facts our people must need to realize. . . . It shows
a fine fearlessness in assailing the popular and mischievous sentimentalities and attractive and corroding
falsehoods which few men dare assail."

Legends, Lies, and Cherished Myths

people descended from the same ancestors, speaking the same language, professing the same religion, attached to the same principles of government, very similar in their manners and customs." The phrase "melting pot" wasn't coined until 1908. It didn't make it into Webster's dictionary until 1934.[6]

Whether Americans in the eighteenth century *should* have thought of themselves as essentially one people is a matter of opinion. While English customs and values seemed preponderant, demographic statistics suggest other cultures may have had a strong influence on the country as well. In 1790 three out of five Americans were not of English origin; two out of five didn't even come from English-speaking backgrounds.[7]

The Frontier

The popular image of the frontier as a place of violence is only partly due to the fact that the place often was violent. Most of it is due to hype, particularly Hollywood hype. The truth is many more people have died in Hollywood westerns than ever died on the real frontier (Indian wars considered apart). In the real Dodge City, for instance, there were just five killings in 1878, the most homicidal year in the little town's frontier history—scarcely enough to sustain a typical two-hour movie. In the most violent year in Deadwood, South Dakota, only four people were killed. In the worst year in Tombstone, home of the shoot-out at the OK Corral, only five people were killed. The only reason the OK Corral shoot-out even became famous was that town boosters deliberately overplayed the drama to attract new settlers. "They eventually cashed in on the tourist boom," historian W. Eugene Hollon says, "by inventing a myth about a town too tough to die."

The most notorious cow towns in Kansas—Abilene, Dodge City, Ellsworth, Wichita, and Caldwell—did see comparatively more violence than similar-size small towns elsewhere but probably not as much violence as is believed. Records indicate that between 1870 and 1885 just forty-five murders occurred in the towns.

Most surprisingly, there is no evidence anyone was ever killed in a frontier shoot-out at high noon.[1]

In fact, few of those who are famous for shooting people shot as many people as is commonly thought. Billy the Kid was a "psychopathic murderer," but he hadn't killed twenty-one people by the time he was twenty-one. Hollon says authorities "can only account for three men he killed for sure, and there were probably no more than three or four more."

Bat Masterson is another overrated killer. He's been credited, says Hollon, with killing between twenty and thirty men; "the actual number was only three."

Wild Bill Hickok, the Abilene marshal, claimed to have killed six Kansas outlaws and secessionists in the incident that first made him famous. He lied. He killed just three—all unarmed. And he never killed anybody for violating the ordinance against firing guns within town limits.

Bill Cody's reputation as a gunslinger often seemed like pure fiction—and was. For it was only in dime novels, which he himself had a hand in writing, that Cody resorted so often to gunfire. As he acknowledged in a letter to his publisher, he didn't care much for the truth. "I am sorry to have to lie so outrageously in this yarn. . . . If you think the revolver and the bowie-knife are used too freely, you may cut out a fatal shot or stab wherever you deem it wise." Cody was a good shot and is said to have proved it repeatedly at the bison-killing contests where he earned the nickname Buffalo Bill. But he didn't kill many Indians, and when he was old his estranged wife revealed he had been wounded in combat with Indians only once, not 137 times as he claimed.[2]

The truth is, few frontiersmen who are remembered for anything are remembered accurately. That's true no matter which frontier era they're from. Of all our frontier heroes, the most confusion many surround the hero who appeared first, John Smith,

The Frontier

of Jamestown fame. Even the story about Pocahontas's saving Smith's life is a matter of dispute. Smith first related the story ten years after it had supposedly happened. When he did, no one stepped forward to corroborate the tale. Furthermore, he told it at a suspiciously opportune moment in 1616, when Pocahontas, then the celebrated wife of Virginia planter John Rolfe, was being courted by the British royal family. Even Smith's defenders admit he probably brought the story up in order to ingratiate himself with the crown. When Pocahontas appeared at court, Smith sent the queen a little book explaining how the young Indian had "hazarded the beating out of her own brains to save mine."[3]

At least John Smith was responsible for most of the myths about John Smith. Most of the myths about Davy Crockett were created not by Crockett but by his political supporters, the Whigs. The politicians published ghostwritten autobiographies to improve Crockett's standing as a frontier hero and as a possible successor to Democrat Andrew Jackson. In one book, recounting his first trip to Washington, Crockett is asked to identify himself. He does so—in his own inimitable way. Why, I'm Davy Crockett, he says. "I'm that same David Crockett, fresh from the backwoods, half-horse, half-alligator, a little touched with the snapping-turtle; can wade the Mississippi, leap the Ohio, ride upon a streak of lightning, and slip without a scratch down a honey locust; can whip my weight in wild cats—and if any gentleman pleases, for a ten-dollar bill, he may throw in a panther."

The true Davy Crockett was neither like the figure in the autobiographies nor like the clean-shaven, soft-talking, bath-taking hero portrayed by Fess Parker in the 1954–55 television series. He wasn't universally popular, he wasn't respectable, and he wasn't the perfect role model for children. When he ran for reelection to Congress in 1835, he was defeated. When he grew disenchanted with his wife, he deserted her. As a child he was a juvenile delinquent. He always had plenty of friends, but he was known as something of an ignoramus. When he claimed to have shot more than a hundred bears, friends reportedly joked that couldn't be. Davy couldn't count that high.[4]

* * *

Of all the frontier figures that are sunk in myth, none are sunk deeper than the Indians. And of all the myths about Indians, the most common is that they were uncommonly savage.

To be sure, Indians did, despite polemical claims to the contrary, invent scalping. Scalping wasn't even known in Europe before the seventeenth century. Linguistic studies indicate that not until the middle 1600's did Europeans have a word for the practice. Indians, in contrast, seem to have begun scalping thousands of years ago. Archaeologists have recently discovered proof of scalping in ancient Indian corpses. Moreover, European explorers reported finding Indians who resorted to the practice as early as the 1500's. It may be thought that the Europeans were not exactly reliable witnesses; but there seems to be no reason to think they made up the reports about Indian rituals involving scalping, including dances and songs, and the rituals bear directly on the truth of the charge. Scholars say Indians created rituals only around ancient behaviors; if the Indians had borrowed scalping from the Europeans, they never would have ritualized the practice.

But it's not as if Europeans abjured the practice. Europeans early sounded a ringing condemnation of scalping, but with the consistency people usually show in such matters, they then adopted the practice themselves. They began by paying Indians to scalp other Indians. When that seemed inadequate to their needs, they hired Indians to scalp other Europeans. Before long Europeans were scalping each other.[5]

While the Indian invented scalping, it was the white man who first conceived of using killer dogs as an instrument of war on the frontier. The dogs—English mastiffs, bred for the specific purpose of killing Indians—weighed a fearsome 150 pounds, stood two and a half feet high, and could rip apart a person with ease. One historian has called the mastiff "an unstoppable engine of war."

Using mastiffs to bait bears and bulls was illegal in many of the English colonies, but Indian baiting was considered both legal and moral. When the crown, out of humanitarian concern, cracked down on the importation of mastiffs to America, colonies like Massachusetts began breeding the dogs, in the words of one law,— to provide for "the Better Security of the Frontiers." Even Benjamin Franklin endorsed Indian baiting. In 1755 Franklin specifically recommended keeping the dogs locked up immediately prior to using them against Indians so "they will be fresher and fiercer for having been previously confin'd, and will confound the Enemy a good deal, and be very serviceable." Some were bothered by the practice but justified it on the ground that it was just retribution. "If the Indians were as other people are, & did manage their warr fairly after the manner of other nations," said Massachusetts Reverend Solomon Stoddard in 1703, "it might be looked upon as inhumane to pursue them in such a manner. But they are to be looked upon as thieves and murderers, they doe acts of hostility without proclaiming war. . . . They act like wolves & are to be dealt withal as wolves."[6]

Besides baiting Indians with dogs, Europeans infected them with smallpox. In what may well have been the first case of biological warfare in history, British General Jeffrey Amherst arranged to give a group of unsuspecting Indians some contaminated blankets taken from a smallpox hospital. Predictably the Indians came down with the disease.[7]

History, of course, is written by the winners, and winners choose to ignore their own violence and to emphasize the violence of the losers.

What if the Indians had written the history books? How different might things appear? Way different.

Indians would probably have pointed out that they didn't just form a backdrop of menace. They were often actually, as one historian has put it, the "principal *determinants* of historical events." James Axtell says that without the Indian, American history would have been far different: White settlement would have proceeded far more quickly; Manifest Destiny might have appeared in the eighteenth century instead of the nineteenth; there wouldn't have been a fur trade (which accounted for 30 to 50 percent of the exports from Pennsylvania and New York in the first half of the

1700's); the English would not have had to worry about the French, who depended on alliances with the Indians; the Revolution would have come later since the British wouldn't have had to send troops over to America to keep peace on the frontier, troops that were a major source of colonial discontent.

The Indians also might have been expected to indicate that their decimation as a people deserves a little coverage. No one knows how many Indians lived in North America when the Europeans came, but it was far more than live here now. By one estimate, as many as eighteen million Indians were present. Axtell conservatively says there were four million. Today there are fewer than one million.[8]

Indians—and Indian sympathizers—are writing history books now from fresh perspectives, but now is a little late. The myths were established when white men wrote the books from the white man's perspective.

Violence aside, the frontier is identified most with individualism, courage, and candor. Individualism no doubt flourished on the frontier, but not precisely in the way many people think. Historians are pretty much agreed that the frontier did not encourage, as Carl Becker puts it in an influential essay on Kansas, the individualism of eccentricity. Indeed, the historical record suggests just the opposite: that frontier society did its best to discourage individuals who wished to be different, whether heathen, heretic, or hell raiser. If anything, a high value was placed on conformity. Those who asserted their uniqueness were apt to be scorned or worse.

Individualism of a different sort, the individualism of achievement, did prevail on the frontier, according to Becker. While the frontier discouraged eccentric behavior, one was taught to lead a life independent of government control and to be self-reliant. "It is not because he fears governmental activity," writes Becker, "but because he has so often had to dispense with it, that the American is an individualist. Altogether averse to hesitancy, doubt, speculative or introspective tendencies, the frontiersman is a man of faith: of faith, not so much in some external power as in himself, in his luck, his destiny; faith in the possibility of achieving whatever is necessary."[9]

Some frontier communities, primarily religious ones, took a downright dim view of individualism, sensibly believing that only by sticking close together could they survive. When the Pilgrims landed in 1620, they immediately put the colony under communal rule, forcing settlers to surrender private supplies for the good of the general welfare. Communism remained alive and well in Plymouth for several years. Mormons experimented with communism, too. Pioneers in parts of Utah pooled their profits; property was held in common. In the early years Mormon church leaders urged members to vote alike on political questions.[10]

That the pioneer was above all else personally courageous is well known, probably true, but not universally believed. James Truslow Adams has suggested that in one very real sense many pioneers were cowards: They chose to run when the going got tough at home rather than fight and take a stand. The road West was difficult and perilous, but it often seemed less hazardous to pioneers than remaining where they were. Adams particularly disdains the Puritans and suggests they left their native land because they lacked the strength to put up with deprivations there. "We think of them as strong men," writes Adams, "but it may be questioned whether those who remained in England, faced the conditions, including possible martydom, and fought the Stuart tyranny to a successful finish were not the stronger."[11]

The assertion that the frontiersman was candid is probably true as regards his personal relations. But it's demonstrably untrue about his architecture, at least in the Old West. Alas for the stereotype, the frontiersman's single contribution to architecture was the "false front," the phony facade added to downtown buildings to give the appearance of a second story. Almost every nineteenth-century western town had one, a source of continuing amusement to city folk, who had nothing to compare with it.

Those who make their livings trying to understand the westerner have been hard put to explain the origin of the false fronts, but they suggest the development may have had something to do

Legends, Lies, and Cherished Myths

with feelings of insecurity. In their view, the false front was a re-assuring sign of confidence in the future at a time when frontier towns had to worry whether they had a future at all. "The false fronts," says Richard Lingeman, "proclaimed that here was a lively business street of a live-wire town—that it was a going concern—and they announced it instantaneously, without drawing any longer looks that would go behind the facade." [12]

The fact is that not only whole towns but whole institutions—even institutions which later seemed to loom so large in the history of the place—came and went quickly on the frontier. The pony express, for example, lasted a mere nineteen months, from April 1860 to October 1861. [13]

The frontier itself, however, lasted and lasted—and much longer than most people suspect. Despite the impression that the frontier ended sometime in the last century, it persisted well into this century. Government records show that more people staked claims to frontier lands under the Homestead Act in 1910 than ever before. [14]

From Slavery
to Freedom

In recent years many of the most offensive myths about black history have been exposed and discredited, but myths remain, some more pernicious than others.

Even so well aired an issue as slavery is still badly misunderstood. This includes one of the most basic subjects of all: Where and when the institution was first outlawed. It wasn't in the North, as might be expected, but in the South, indeed, in the Deep South, in the colony of Georgia, in 1735. Three years after Georgia was founded, its trustees forbade the introduction of blacks into the colony (the only colony ever to do so) for the express purpose of forestalling the development of slavery.

The issue is complicated by the fact that slavery was excluded not out of concern for blacks but to help whites. The founders worried that slavery would be incompatible with the goal of establishing Georgia as a refuge for debtors who wanted a new start in life. It was particularly feared that the institution would lead to the subjugation of the majority of settlers, who couldn't afford to buy slaves of their own.

Those fears were well founded. Fifteen years after blacks were banned, the trustees, under pressure from big planters, reversed themselves and approved the importation of slaves. Within a few short years the dreaded subjugation of debtor whites ensued, just as had been predicted.[1]

Confusion is widespread not only about slavery but about the slave trade. The foreign slave trade was abolished nationwide in 1808, as everyone knows, but it hadn't exactly been left alone before then. As early as colonial times steps were taken to abolish or curtail the trade in Delaware, Massachusetts, and Virginia. Delaware outlawed the importation of slaves; Massachusetts tried to do the same but was overruled by the royal governor; Virginia denounced the trade and asked the crown to curtail it. In 1776 the Second Continental Congress resolved that "no slaves be imported into any of the Thirteen United Colonies." In 1777 the crown ordered an end to the immigration of all blacks, free and slave.*[2]

More serious than the misperceptions about the slave trade are those about emancipation. Children thrill to stories about Lincoln's Emancipation Proclamation, but his wasn't the first. The first was issued by a most unlikely liberator, the British royal governor of Virginia, Lord Dunmore, in 1775. In a shrewd move designed to make trouble for the Virginia patriots, many of whom were slaveholders, Dunmore promised to free any black willing to take up arms for the British government. Within weeks eight hundred slaves had taken up the offer and were given their freedom. George Washington became so alarmed he warned friends that if Dunmore were not crushed by spring, "he will become the most formidable enemy America has. His forces will increase like a Snow Ball rolling if some expedient cannot be hit upon to convince the Slaves and Servants of the impotency of his Design."

---

*No one knows precisely how many blacks were imported to the colonies and the United States, but there were far fewer than were imported to the rest of the Americas. One researcher has found that we imported some 425,000 blacks from Africa—about 4.5 percent of the total imported to the Western Hemisphere via the Atlantic slave trade. Only here did the black population grow naturally. In every other slave society deaths so exceeded births that the only way to keep up the black population was to keep importing blacks. "In no other slave society, in fact, did the number surviving at the end of slavery come near equaling the number originally imported" (see C. Vann Woodward, *Thinking Back* [1986], p. 128).

Washington need not have worried. Before more slaves were freed, the Dunmore offer was withdrawn under pressure from the authorities in London, who believed the proclamation needlessly antagonized southerners who might yet be persuaded to remain in the empire. Of those who had been freed, few survived long enough to do the patriots much harm. Crammed aboard ships anchored in Norfolk Harbor, more than half came down with smallpox. Too few survived healthy enough to fight. Unable to field a large enough army to retake the colony, Dunmore fled, leaving Washington and the rebels in charge.

Some historians have alleged that Washington's response to the Dunmore proclamation proves the hypocrisy of the rebels, who were crying for liberty for themselves while reinforcing slavery for blacks. As the late Jonathan Clark put it in an essay in 1976, the Dunmore incident showed the willingness of the rebels to accept evils that "grossly" contradicted their own ideals.

Skeptics may wonder. In the midst of war the rebels could hardly have been expected to look kindly on attempts by the enemy to recruit their slaves as soldiers, so of course, they regarded Dunmore's plan as diabolical. Later, when it proved possible, they themselves acted to bring slaves into the war effort, though that obviously put the institution in jeopardy. In 1777 several northern states encouraged white masters to free their slaves for military service. Washington himself eventually allowed free blacks to enlist in his army. In 1778 Washington's liberal aide-de-camp John Laurens asked for the right to lead an army of liberated slaves on a campaign through the South. The Continental Congress unanimously approved the plan and authorized Laurens to recruit up to three thousand slaves in South Carolina and Georgia. However, the Laurens plan was never put into effect because of opposition from South Carolina.[3]

They may have been hypocrites to hold slaves and preach freedom, but the founders were not blind to the contradictions. After they won the war, they took repeated steps to limit the institution. In the North a number of states abolished slavery outright. The national legislature forbade slavery in the Northwest Territory

(1787). Some southerners, including Washington, took measures that undermined slavery. When he left the presidency, Washington secretly left several slaves behind in Pennsylvania so they could automatically become free under the state's emancipation law. When he drafted his will, he provided for the freedom of the rest of his slaves upon his wife's death.

Opposition to slavery was not confined to northerners. Historian Carl Degler in a pathbreaking book points out that at times there were more groups opposed to slavery in the South than in the North. Occasionally these opponents of slavery, members of the "other South," very nearly succeeded in abolishing the institution. Their most sensational effort was made in the Virginia legislature in 1832. The vote came after a two-week debate on slavery that was sparked by the death of fifty-seven whites during Nat Turner's Rebellion. The abolitionists lost, of course, but they showed surprising strength. Fifty-three legislators voted to abolish slavery; seventy-three, to keep it. A motion to condemn slavery as an evil lost by just seven votes. In his diary Governor John Floyd confided his desire to get rid of the institution: "Before I leave this Government I will have contrived to have a law passed gradually abolishing slavery in this state, or at all events to begin the work of prohibiting slavery on the west side of the Blue Ridge Mountains."[4]

That southerners actually thought blacks liked slavery is widely believed but dubious. Early movies often gave us the image of the beaming plantation owner warming to the antics of his carefree, lovable, and clownish slaves. But while planters may have harbored genuine familial feelings for their slaves, they frequently lived in fear of them, particularly in places where blacks outnumbered whites and even more particularly after Turner's Rebellion. Southern legislators, alert to the dangers all around them, enacted reams of laws designed to keep slaves in check. It should be evident that laws forbidding the teaching of slaves to read and write, for instance, would hardly have been necessary if whites had really thought blacks were content and happy.

Among themselves, slaveholders complained frequently about

123
From Slavery to Freedom

their "shrewd and cunning" slaves. Masters who dealt daily with slaves pretty soon learned that they had to be careful not to be taken in by blacks who pretended to blindness, paralysis, and the like to escape work. As the foreign observer Harriet Martineau discovered on her famous tour of the southern states, the "endearing relation" that appeared to prevail between master and slave covered a relationship based on distrust and loathing.

The myth of the slave's contentment seems to have been caused by the master's need to justify the system to himself and to others. Not coincidentally, it appeared most frequently in the 1850's, just when the institution came under the most severe attacks. Some have suggested the myth was designed chiefly for northern consumption, but it may be it was most useful in reassuring southerners of the justice of their cause.

More distressing are the still-prevalent beliefs that blacks endured slavery without protest and the unspoken assumption that whites never would have. The fact is that blacks didn't idly tolerate their own oppression any more than whites would have. Three times in the antebellum period blacks conspired to overthrow their masters in large-scale and imaginative rebellions. In 1800 Gabriel Prosser organized an army of a thousand slaves and, on August 30, boldly led them on a march to take Richmond; only the quick action of the state militia, which had been alerted by a turncoat, prevented a general bloodletting. Afterward dozens of slaves were arrested, and the thirty-five executed included Prosser, who was killed after refusing to implicate his coconspirators. In 1822 Denmark Vesey plotted to seize Charleston but was turned in by an informer and arrested along with thirty-five other blacks. The most serious revolt occurred in 1831 under Nat Turner and resulted in the execution of more than a hundred blacks.

One suspects it wouldn't have done the Negro much good if he had won a reputation for militancy rather than servility. When in the 1960's he began frequently turning to violence, he earned many people's enmity, but not their respect. It may be that the black man only could have won the esteem of racists if, like the North American Indian, he had proved impossible to enslave and

had died in the process. In the racists' lexicon, self-inflicted genocide would have been morally superior to survival.

The comparison with the Indians is, by the way, based on an
old fallacy. It is supposed that Indians as a people could not be
enslaved. The truth is that only North American Indians—largely
nomadic—proved resistant. Indians in Latin America who came
from strong agricultural communities were often enslaved successfully by the Spanish and Portuguese.[5]

The racist claim that blacks acquiesced in slavery is usually
accompanied by the claim that slaves were not particularly good
employees. Inevitably this is given as further evidence of the blacks'
inferiority, but it actually demonstrates, as recent historians have
observed, the slaves' daily rebellion against their masters. Breaking
farm implements, stealing white property, and, of course, running
away frequently demonstrated the slaves' contempt for their masters. Every day wasted away was, therefore, evidence not of lazi-
ness but rather of rebellion. Some slaves surely were lazy, but why
shouldn't they have been? What stake did they have in the success
of the system?[6]

Among the most common myths about blacks and slavery,
three stem from the Civil War era and have to do with *Uncle
Tom's Cabin*, the Underground Railroad, and the position of slavery in the Confederacy.

That Harriet Beecher Stowe's Uncle Tom was despicable and
sniveling is widely believed but utterly illusory. Stowe's fictional
Uncle Tom was no Uncle Tom. He was kindly, considerate, hu-
mane, and brave. When Simon Legree orders Uncle Tom to flog
a slave who's too sick to work, the old slave refuses: "[T]his yer
thing I can't feel it right to do;—and mas'r. I *never* shall do it—
never! . . . I'll die first." Unmoved, Legree orders Tom whipped
practically to death. Tom never relents—at least not in Stowe's
telling of the tale. In the plays based on her book, though, plays
that were staged hundreds of times for northern audiences, Tom
is subservient and spineless. Only in the book is he noble.[7]

The Underground Railroad is the source of numerous inspir-
ing stories, almost none of them true. The idea that the Under-

ground Railroad saved up to a hundred thousand slaves has been repeated endlessly (as in earlier editions of the *Encyclopædia Britannica*) but ignorantly. The old figures are based on the claims of the abolitionists, and modern scholarship says the abolitionists' estimate of a hundred thousand rescues was wildly inflated. Historians now suggest maybe a few thousand slaves at best were helped to freedom by the Underground Railroad.

Odder still, in light of the hullabaloo about the Underground Railroad, is the scholar's discovery that the railroad wasn't much help even to those few thousand who were able to use it. While the assistance of a railroad conductor was always welcome, the conductor was in a position to help the slave only after he'd already made the most dangerous part of the journey himself—that which took the slave out of the South and into a border state where the railroad operated.

The reason for the error is that the history books were written by whites, and whites naturally thought their own efforts were the most important. As the abolitionists saw it, the blacks were the passive recipients of white aid. Except for Harriet Tubman, no black was given credit for rescuing blacks.[8]

The position of slavery under the Confederacy is believed well known but isn't. Slavery underwent fantastic changes during the war and was the object of repeated attempts at reform while the war lasted. Among other things, reformers proposed outlawing the sale of slave children and allowing slave testimony to be heard in court (it never had been). In Alabama in 1864 several enacted reform measures included a law requiring masters to get legal counsel when their slaves were indicted for major criminal offenses.

Slavery not only may have been changing but may well have been dying. Early in the war Confederate wives, left to tend the plantations alone while their husbands were off fighting, began to complain that their once-docile slaves had become "uppity." After Lincoln issued the Emancipation Proclamation, slaves became downright ornery, refusing to do chores even when threatened with beatings. Confederates despaired of ever being able to restore the old ways even if they won the war. "The faithful slave is about played out," wrote one. "They are the most treacherous, brutal, and ungrateful race on the globe."

Another southerner told her husband, "You may give your negroes away if you won't hire them, and I'll move into a white settlement and work with my hands." Few slaves staged outright revolts, but thousands ran away. In the single month of January 1864 Jefferson Davis himself lost three slaves, one of whom tried burning down the executive mansion on his way out.

Surprising as it may be to learn that slavery was in trouble in the Confederacy, the real shocker may be that Confederate leaders themselves considered abolishing the institution. Just a month before the collapse of his government Jefferson Davis authorized one of his diplomats in Europe to inform Britain and France that the Confederacy was willing to emancipate the South's slaves in exchange for official recognition as an independent country. That very month the Confederate Congress, at the request of General Robert E. Lee, authorized the recruitment of up to three hundred thousand slaves into the army. Lee told the Congress that black troops were essential to winning the war. So desperate were southerners that a Mississippi newspaper published an editorial in favor of abolitionism. "Let not slavery prove a barrier to our independence," said the Jackson *Mississippian*. "If it is found in the way— if it proves an insurmountable object of the achievement of our liberty and separate nationality, away with it! Let it perish!"[9]

The paradox is that the South probably couldn't win the war to save slavery without abolishing or modifying the institution. In the end southern leaders seemed willing to do that, but by then it was too late.

Some of the most popular errors about black history stem from the Reconstruction period. Of these, probably the most vulgar and the one that has done the most mischief is the idea that blacks can't be trusted with power. Among other things it is claimed that blacks pillaged the Confederate treasuries, impoverished the well-to-do with high taxes, disfranchised whites so as to be able to take complete charge (as one racist writer put it, because blacks be-

From Slavery to Freedom

lieved "We'se de winnin' culler"), took over the legislatures of the South and many governorships, and elected subliterate and ignorant politicians to high office.

Some whites have charged that blacks became so unruly even their northern friends turned against them. Claude Bowers echoed this view in his popular 1929 account of Reconstruction *The Tragic Era*: "Even Northerners, not prone to sympathize with the prostrate foe, were shocked and humiliated by the scenes they saw. In the streets and highways they took no pride in the spectacle of thousands of blacks with muskets and shimmering bayonets swaggering in jeering fashion before their former masters and mistresses."

The fact is that in only two states, South Carolina and Georgia, did blacks form a majority of the legislatures during Reconstruction. In those states blacks happened to outnumber whites in the general population. No blacks were elected governor. Only in South Carolina was there even a single black Supreme Court Justice. At every constitutional convention save two, blacks were in the minority—whites had the major hand in writing the provisions for suffrage. To be sure, taxes increased after the war, but they had to, to pay for the hundreds of new schools built for blacks who had never had schools before.

As for the claim that the Reconstruction governments were corrupt, there's ample evidence this was so. But it needs to be remembered, and rarely is, that governments everywhere in the United States were corrupt during this period. This was, after all, in Twain's phrase, the Gilded Age. In New York there was Tammany Hall; in Washington, D.C., the Crédit Mobilier scandal. Railroad barons ruled California; steel magnates dominated Pennsylvania politics, often illegally. Yet no one ever suggested northern whites proved by their behavior they couldn't be trusted with power. Such slander was reserved for blacks alone.[10]

Perhaps out of a sense of fair play, blacks have been considered not just villains but victims, too; both enemies and friends alike have suggested at times that slavery destroyed the black family.

There is no evidence that this is true. That the black family is in trouble now almost no one denies. But slavery may not be directly to blame. The latest scholarship insists that the black family began coming apart only in this century, under the pressure of urban problems and racism. In slavery times it all but flourished. Eugene D. Genovese, a Marxist historian who has studied the black slave family more deeply probably than any other person, was struck by the strength of family bonds. He has pointed out that when cruel masters separated husbands and wives, the couples often ran away to try to remain together. "Next to resentment over punishment," he writes, "the attempt to find relatives was the most prevalent cause of flight." One of the very first things blacks did after being emancipated was to seek out lost relatives on other plantations. After the war thousands rushed out to legalize marriages made unofficially under slavery. Family ties were so strong that whites began complaining because blacks refused to send their children away to be apprenticed. In short, says Genovese, despite what you might think, the black family not only endured slavery but survived the institution intact.[11]

Genovese's conclusion is confirmed by census studies compiled by the late Herbert Gutman. Until the 1920's, Gutman found, the typical black household "had in it two parents and was not 'unorganized or disorganized.'" Gutman reported it wasn't until after the 1920's that the black family started disintegrating. He suggested the breakup may have had to do with the mass migration of rural southern blacks to cities in the North. As he pointed out, here was dislocation on a grand and unprecedented scale. Driven from the land, blacks discovered they couldn't find work or make money in the cities, and without money the family shattered. From the Great Depression right up through the present, black unemployment has remained singularly high; for every unemployed white person, there have been two unemployed blacks.

The belief that Negro inferiority, not slavery, is to blame for the failure of the black family is one of the old racist libels that one still hears, though less than in earlier times. In its original form at the turn of the century the argument took on a blatantly

From Slavery to Freedom

hostile tone, though advocates claimed to be speaking the language of objective social science. A psychologist, James Cattell, in an article in *Popular Science Monthly* in 1903, indicated, in a startlingly crude fashion, that "a savage brought up in a cultivated society will not only retain his dark skin, but is also likely to have the incoherent mind of his race."

Another social scientist, Howard Odum, one of the best known in the South, claimed even further limitation. "The negro," he wrote, "has little home conscience or love of home, no local attachments of the better sort. . . . He has no pride of ancestry, and he is not influenced by the lives of great men. . . . He has little conception of the meaning of virtue, truth, honor, manhood, integrity. . . . They [blacks] sneer at the idea of work. . . . Their moral natures are miserably perverted."

Less encompassing but more provocative than these accusations was the old argument that sexuality was to blame for the problems of the black family. In a study heavily laden with scientific jargon, a physical anthropologist concluded that the black's problem was the "instability of character incident to lack of self-control, especially in connection with the sexual relation." Translated, that meant black males couldn't make good husbands because they couldn't keep their pants flies closed.

Of all the racist claims none has done more mischief or seemed more unanswerable to true believers than the charge that only blacks—among the nation's long-settled minorities—never made it. Despite anti-Semitism Jews made it. So did Italians, the Irish, and others. So why not blacks?

Blacks, in answer, blame racism. Racist whites resort to malicious talk about black inferiority.

Both are wrong. Blacks have made it, though maybe not as far as others. And they have made it faster than almost any other minority group ever has *once they began the climb up.* The climb up didn't begin until relatively recent times, however. The starting date is 1950. In that year, according to the federal census records, about 10 percent of American blacks ranked in the middle class. Just a decade later 18 percent did. By 1970, more than a third of

American blacks had joined the American middle class. Professor Richard C. Wade, reviewing these data, concludes: "The size of this black middle class is large; indeed, no other group has had a success story equal to it." *

Mystery surrounds the transformation. Some have suggested, as a reviewer in the *New York Times Book Review* did in 1987, that along with the postwar boom, which made whites less resistant to black progress, the civil rights movement deserves part of the credit. Perhaps. But most of the improvement in the position of blacks occurred before the civil rights movement had a chance to have much of an impact.[12]

---

*Some other groups, like the Vietnamese, have climbed faster than blacks. But comparing their progress with that of blacks isn't exactly fair. Though they may have started out poor, they usually didn't start out unskilled. Blacks usually did.

From Slavery to Freedom

Education

The popular belief that we currently don't educate our children very well but could if only we tried hard enough rests in part on a legend that once upon a time we did educate them well. People are a little vague about when this golden age existed—perhaps earlier in this century—but there's no doubt it did exist, whenever it was!

And how well we did the job! The school was so effective it could take the foreign language-speaking son of an immigrant peddler and in no time at all turn him into a happy, productive, English-speaking American professional. With a little luck the kid might even become a doctor or lawyer. It didn't matter what his ethnic background was, whether Irish, Italian, or Jewish; the school bestowed its blessings democratically, without regard to race, creed, or color. Neither caste nor class played a role; all were treated equally.

Yet we have it on good authority that the school of legend did not exist—at least not in the early decades of this century, when it was presumably doing so much to help immigrant children become good Americans. Colin Greer has established that more students failed than succeeded in schools during just the time when the schools were supposedly doing such a crack job. Greer says that several studies conclusively show that most students in the schools of Chicago, New York, Boston, Detroit, Philadelphia, and Pittsburgh could not read, write, or do 'rithmetic at their grade levels.

A striking illustration of the failure of the schools was the dropout rate that prevailed in the 1920's and 1930's. A federal study of students across the country in that twenty-year period showed that only 56 percent graduated from high school. In individual cities the rate was often far lower. In New York City only 40 percent graduated. In the twenties in Philadelphia only 19 percent of those entering high school managed to finish. Even in the 1940's things did not improve much; in Boston, for example, fully 50 percent of the ninth graders failed to complete high school.

Remarkable as these statistics are, it might take something more to persuade Americans that the early-twentieth-century school was less effective than imagined. Perhaps a trip through time to a school in New York would do. What would we find? We would expect to see cleanly scrubbed children, quietly seated at neat rows of wooden desks equipped with filled inkwells. In truth, if we had chanced upon the hundreds of schools catering to the children of immigrants, say, at the turn of the century, we would find squalor equal to the worst tenements from which the children came. Like the tenements, the schools would be overcrowded. Worse, the stench and filth would be overpowering. A rat might even cross our path, though it would be hard to notice in such poorly lighted classrooms. If we happened along on the right day, we might run into Jacob Riis, the reformer, on one of his fact-collecting missions. The inner city school was high on the reformer's list of Things That Needed to Be Improved.[1]

Whether the public school at the start of the century was better or worse than it had been previously is unclear. Things may have been worse. In the 1890's, according to the federal government, only slightly more than half the children in America entered school at all. Nonwhites in particular stayed away from school in droves; only 33 percent were ever enrolled.[2]

Among institutions of learning, colleges, Harvard especially, also figure in myth. Harvard has for so much of this century demonstrated academic excellence that it is believed to have done so always. When Harvard celebrated its 350th anniversary in 1986, the rest of the country joined in; the university even found itself on the cover of *Time*. Harvardians naturally thought the attention well deserved. But why the rest of the country put up with the illusion that Harvard ought to be celebrating *all* of its 350 years is puzzling.

There is, for instance, the curious matter of the way Harvard ranked students during much of its history. While in the seventeenth century students were ranked according to academic standing, in the next century the college began ranking them according to family status, those at the top of the social heap placing at the top of the class. In the nineteenth century things improved, but not by much. Academic achievement again began to be taken into consideration, but rank was also determined by a student's behavior. Among other things, demerits affecting student rank were given for late attendance at prayers (sixteen points), lying on the grass (sixteen points), shouting from a window in the yard (sixteen points), playing a musical instrument in study period (sixteen points). Students interested in the academic side of college life frequently became demoralized since points for a good paper could easily be offset by demerits, say, for lounging. The result, predictably, as Edward Everett Hale complained, was that students became indifferent to college rank. Not until 1868 did the college agree (quoting a Harvard resolution) to keep "the scales of scholarship and conduct" distinct.

College rank aside, there is the question of the quality of teaching at Harvard. One assumes it was high. Yet the evidence suggests that even many of Harvard's own teachers thought it wasn't. Among other things, teachers regularly complained they were overwhelmed by the work load. This isn't an unusual complaint as far as college teachers are concerned, of course, but it seems to have been made with especially good reason at Harvard in the last century. Even the great and learned Henry Adams complained he could not keep up with the demands. After he was hired, he was astonished to learn it would be up to him to teach all of Western history that fell between the courses taught by two other professors, a period of about a thousand years. Even Adams was a bit daunted by the prospect, though he managed to retain his sense of humor. "There is a pleasing excitement," he wrote friends, "in having to lecture tomorrow on a period of history which I have not heard of till today. . . . Thus far the only merit of my instruction has been its originality, one hundred youths at any rate have learned facts and theories for which in after life they will hunt the authorities in vain, unless, as I trust, they forget all they have been told."

College teachers in general in the nineteenth century, by the way, were often inferior to their twentieth-century counterparts. When Charles William Eliot took over the presidency of Harvard in 1869, he complained that "very few Americans of eminent ability" became college teachers. "The pay has been too low," he observed, "and there has been no gradual rise out of drudgery, such as may reasonably be expected in other callings." Henry Ward Beecher, putting the problem more colorfully, commented: "Who ever heard of a college professor that was not poor? They dry up in a pocket like springs after the wood is cut off from the hills. They are apt to get very dry in other ways, too. A man that teaches cannot afford to know too much."[3]

As for college students, they gave rise to a number of interesting myths, the most important of which may be the belief that students never engaged in major rebellions until the 1960's. History is replete with examples of student rebellions at least as turbulent as the uprisings associated with the Vietnam War generation. In 1830 students at Yale revolted over a change in the teaching of mathematics in an incident dubbed the "Conic Section's Rebellion." Before it was over, forty-three students —about half of the class—had been expelled. In ensuing years tensions remained so high that some students came to school armed with dangerous weapons. Earlier, in 1818 and again in 1828, Yale students revolted against the food; both times the situations became so severe the administration was forced to close the school down. One Christmas students became so destructive they went on a rampage, smashing windows in buildings across the campus. Professors in turn had to use axes to smash down the doors of several buildings which the students had mischievously locked up.

Yale wasn't the only college in the nineteenth century to be struck by student violence. Historians say that at Princeton between 1800 and 1830 there were no fewer than six student insurrections. And at Harvard things got so bad several buildings were partially blown up; a Harvard leader observed that students frequently committed "crimes that were worthy of the penitentiary." At the University of Virginia in 1836 student militants, illegally armed with guns, engaged in mob violence so severe that the school had to ask for the help of armed soldiers. In 1840 a University of Virginia professor who angered his students was killed.[4]

Related to myths about schoolteachers and college students are long-held beliefs about school reference books, chiefly the *Encyclopædia Britannica*. Long regarded as voluminous, impressive, and exhaustive, the old red-bound reference work was frequently inaccurate, obsolete, and embarrassingly incomplete. Generations of students who venerated the *Britannica* knew not what they revered. Harvey Einbinder, who conducted a systematic study of the encyclopedia, reports that only the eleventh edition, published in 1910–11, fulfilled the work's promise.

Among Einbinder's findings is the discovery that the 1958 edition was anything but up-to-date. Many of the chief essays were forty years old or older. Biographies of Percy Shelley, Thomas Macaulay, and Walter Scott had first appeared in the ninth edition—seventy-five years earlier. Demographic figures of key Polish cities hadn't been updated since 1931, leaving the misimpression that Jews, for example, still accounted for half the population of Tarnopol. An essay on the classics insisted that the study of Latin and

Greek was flourishing "as vigorously as it has done at any time." The essay went on to say: "So far as the evidence goes, the prospects of classical scholarship as an indispensable force in education appear to be singularly bright." Comments Einbinder: "Perhaps this explains why the entry on Cicero contains eight lines of Latin and the article on Sophocles four lines of Greek without translation."[5]

Holidays

I n the willingness of Americans to foster myth and misconception, nothing is sacred, not even holidays.

That American independence was declared on the Fourth of July in 1776 is so well established that it might seem unpatriotic to question the fact. But it's not fact. Historical records plainly show that independence was declared by the Continental Congress in Philadelphia on July 2. The night of the second the Pennsylvania *Evening Post* published the statement: "This day the Continental Congress declared the United Colonies Free and Independent States."

Americans have endeavored not to let the facts get in the way of tradition, however. When a scholar in the nineteenth century discovered a John Adams letter that contradicted the tradition of the Fourth of July, he simply altered the document to conform with current belief. Adams had predicted in a letter to his wife dated July 3, 1776, that from then on "the Second day of July, 1776, will be the most memorable Epocha, in the History of

America. I am apt to believe that it will be celebrated, by succeeding Generations, as the great anniversary Festival." To "correct" the record, the scholar altered the date of the document to read "July 5" and had Adams predicting that the holiday would be celebrated, not on the second but on the fourth.

The widespread belief in the Fourth as the great anniversary day is based on the fact that Jefferson's Declaration of Independence was adopted that day; when the declaration was published, it bore the date July 4. Thus what seems to have happened, as one scholar observed, is that the document announcing independence overshadowed the act of declaring it. Congress itself didn't celebrate independence until July 8, when the members participated in a gala public demonstration that included the firing of guns and a parade of soldiers. People in the rest of the country celebrated independence even later, depending on when the news of Congress's action reached them. Washington's soldiers, camped in New York, didn't hear of the Declaration until July 9. Savannah, Georgia, had to wait until August 10. Word didn't reach London for another two weeks. France finally heard on August 30.

Yet another myth persists concerning the Declaration of Independence: that it was signed the day it was adopted. Even contemporaries got this wrong. Just a few years after the Revolution both Jefferson and Franklin reported in letters to friends their memory that the Declaration had been signed by all of the delegates (with one exception) on July 4. When someone challenged his memory in the early 1800's, Jefferson stuck by his mistake. It wasn't until 1884 that the record was corrected when historian Mellon Chamberlain, researching the manuscript minutes of the journal of Congress, discovered that the declaration was signed by most delegates on August 2. A few didn't affix their signatures until even later. One person didn't sign until 1781. Only John Hancock, president of Congress, and Charles Thomson, secretary, signed it on the fourth. When the document was originally published, the Congress cautiously refused to say who, beyond Hancock and Thomson, had approved it. Not until January 1777 were the names of the other signers released.[1]

Equally wrong is the belief that independence was unanimously supported in Congress. Actually, more than half a dozen delegates opposed the rebellion. In the penultimate roll call Pennsylvania and South Carolina voted no, Delaware's delegates were divided, and New York's members, lacking instructions, didn't vote. In the end South Carolina, Pennsylvania, and Delaware voted to approve independence, South Carolina only because it didn't want to be left out. New York, still uninstructed, abstained.

At least independence is not so shrouded in error as it once was. For a long time North Carolinians believed that they deserved the credit for making the first statement of independence. So convinced were they of the authenticity of the so-called Mecklenburg Declaration of Independence, which was supposedly approved in 1775 in Mecklenburg County, that the state legislature required students to learn about it. In a sober moment the legislature repealed the order. Nothing much has been said about the North Carolina declaration since.

Historian Allan Nevins, apparently with good reason, says it was a fraud. It was not put into written form until 1800, it wasn't even printed until 1820, and its written version was provided by a county clerk on the basis of his memory of the event.[2]

Mecklenburg does figure in the developing schism with Great Britain. In May 1775 some resolutions were passed denying the authority of the king in North Carolina. But there was no mention of independence.*

Thanksgiving is the source of bountiful misconceptions. Though we celebrate this holiday in November, no one knows precisely when the first Thanksgiving took place since none of the surviving Pilgrim records say anything more than that it occurred in the autumn of 1621. At any rate, the holiday was not an annual

---

*Some North Carolinians, smarting over the Mecklenburg fraud, maintain that they still deserve recognition as the first to declare independence. The claim is based on a meeting in Halifax, where the delegates to the Congress were instructed to "concur with the delegates of the other Colonies in declaring Independency." The meeting was held in April 1776. North Carolinian James Street insisted that this "was the first explicit declaration by any Colony in favor of complete separation from Britain." (See Street's *The Revolutionary War* [1954], p. 79.)

Pilgrim event. It was not even firmly fixed as a fall festival. In 1623, according to one scholar's best estimate, it was celebrated in July.

More surprising, the first Thanksgiving wasn't a family celebration. More like a huge community picnic, it lasted for about a week and was attended by more than ninety Indians. Above all, it was an occasion for celebration and recreation. Scholars say it wasn't a religious holiday. The Pilgrims wouldn't have tolerated festivities at a truly religious time.

Whether turkeys were eaten is anybody's guess. Plymouth Colony Governor William Bradford's journal doesn't say one way or the other. Neither do any others.

Opinion is divided about the other things they ate. Robert Myers asserts confidently that they had duck, goose, seafood, eels, white bread, corn bread, leeks, watercress, a variety of greens, and, for dessert, wild plums and dried berries. Roland Usher says they had hasty pudding. Where Myers and Usher came by their information, they don't say. Actually, all that is known for sure is that the Pilgrims had "fowl" and "deer."[3]

Of all holidays, Christmas looms largest on the national calendar, but it hasn't always been in this position. Until the Civil War Christmas was but scantly observed. Most shockingly, retailers hardly seemed to take notice of the occasion. Historians report that the pages of the New York *Tribune* in 1841 did not contain a single example of advertising with a Christmas theme. It wasn't until after the Civil War that retailers began experimenting with special Christmas sales. Once they did, however, it didn't take long for them to discover the commercial possibilities offered by the holiday. By 1870 December had become the merchants' single largest selling month of the year.

Christmas had not, by the way, always been regarded as a proper time for celebration. In the seventeenth century this holiday, which was to become so American, was widely regarded in New England as an unappealing popish import. The leaders of the Massachusetts Bay Colony so disdained Christmas that in 1659 they passed a law against celebrating the holiday, punishing "anybody who is found observing [it], by abstinence from labor, feasting, or any other way." The law was repealed twenty-five years later, but the prejudice against Christmas remained strong. Judge Samuel Sewall was happy to report in his diary in 1685 that he didn't see anybody celebrating the holiday.[4]

Shrines

Many of America's most famous shrines and landmarks are phony. Yet such is the average person's confidence in physical objects that few shrines ever fall under suspicion.

Of all American shrines, perhaps none is more sacred than the Liberty Bell, which, as everyone knows, was rung when independence was declared on July 4, 1776. The only question, when questions are raised, is about the details. One author wrote that the bell was rung by an "old man" with white hair at the signal of a boy with "blue eyes," who had just received word that the delegates had voted for liberty. More colorful narrators recalled that the old man rang the bell a hundred times while crying loudly, "Liberty throughout the land, unto the inhabitants thereof." B. W. Belisle in his *History of Independence Hall*, published in 1859, added the interesting detail that the "gray headed patriot" rang the bell to the cheer of a crowd below, which had "anxiously awaited" the signing of the declaration "with trembling hope."

Such is the popular fascination with the Liberty Bell that a few years ago a group of industrious citizens had full-size replicas of the shrine made up for every state in the Union, so that people who couldn't travel to Philadelphia could benefit from the uplifting sight. In Utah the replica stands just outside the state's House of Representatives. Tour guides point to the bell with reverence, and it's only a duplicate.

Yet the Liberty Bell is a fraud. The story told to millions is twaddle. Experts say the tale is the fabrication of a young nineteenth-century Philadelphian, George Lippard.* Lippard published the story in the aptly titled *Legends of the American Revolution* (1847), a book which catapulted him immediately to the front rank of historical mythmakers.

Of the true story of the Liberty Bell, little is known. It was installed in Independence Hall in 1753. But there is no evidence the bell was rung when independence was declared. In any case, it wouldn't have been rung on the fourth to celebrate the event. Independence was declared on July 2, not July 4. It might have been rung on July 8, when Congress publicly celebrated independence for the first time, but there's no evidence of it.

It is a good-looking bell, but it wasn't a shrine until Lippard. In 1828 the city of Philadelphia even tried to sell it for scrap. There were no takers, however.

The bell contains the inscription "Proclaim Liberty throughout all the Land unto the Inhabitants Thereof." But the inscription, cast when the bell was produced in 1753, had nothing to do with the Revolution.

It is called the Liberty Bell but wasn't named until long after the Revolution—and not in honor of the Revolution. The "liberty" referred to in the title was intended to mean the liberty of blacks, not whites. The name was coined in 1839 by antislavery activists.[1]

Of other shrines associated with historical milestones, Bunker Hill and Plymouth Rock are perhaps subject to the most confusion

---

*Lippard's only other major claim is that he wrote a play considered so racy it was banned by Philadelphia.

and error. Bunker Hill owes its famous reputation to a case of mistaken identity. The famous battle actually took place on Breed's Hill, a smaller mound nearby. The patriots had been under orders to secure Bunker Hill but decided for unknown reasons to throw up their redoubts on Breed's, which, unfortunately, was much more vulnerable to attack. Like those patriots, Americans since have been confused over where the battle took place. So have the British. A British map of Boston made after the battle shows the American forces clearly camped on "Bunkers [sic] Hill."

The Americans, incidentally, lost the Battle of Bunker Hill. After fighting off the more highly trained enemy, the patriots at last gave up and fled, allowing the British to take the hill. British victory, however, came at a frightening cost: more than a thousand royal troops killed and wounded. The Americans suffered five hundred casualties.[2]

The belief that the Pilgrims landed at Plymouth Rock rests solely on dubious secondhand testimony given by a ninety-five-year-old man more than a century after the *Mayflower* arrived. The statement was made in 1741 by Elder Thomas Faunce, who based his claims on a story he had supposedly been told as a boy by his father, who himself arrived in America three years *after* the *Mayflower*.

At any rate, the Pilgrims didn't first land at Plymouth. They landed at Provincetown. To the considerable dismay of the residents of Provincetown, however, nobody remembers that.[3]

Plymouth was not, by the way, the first European settlement in North America, or even the first permanent settlement. Jamestown, planted in 1607, was first. The Pilgrims have won the reputation that they were first only because New England historians made such a fuss about them. And until the nineteenth century American history was largely written of, by, and for New Englanders. Their original bias endures.

Also subject to myth and error are famous homes associated with Lincoln, Betsy Ross, and Stephen Foster. So established is the reputation of the little log cabin on display near Hodgenville, Kentucky, in which Lincoln is said to have been born that it has become a major tourist attraction. It is guarded by the Interior Department and is officially registered as the "Abraham Lincoln Birthplace Historical Site."

It is a fraud, however, as Lincoln's own son Robert attested. Records indicate the original log cabin where Lincoln was born was actually destroyed by fire before 1840. Further, not even the burned logs were saved. According to the reminiscences of an eighty-four-year-old Kentuckian whose family lived in the original cabin, "the logs were burned for firewood." In 1865, the year of Lincoln's death, eyewitnesses reported that there were no signs of a log cabin at the site of the old Lincoln farm where the President had been born.

The fake cabin was built out of logs salvaged from a two-story home near Lincoln's. In an obvious attempt to cash in on the legendary President, the builder, one John Davenport, first advertised it as Lincoln's birthplace, then sold it to Alfred W. Dennett, a promoter. Dennett removed the cabin to Nashville, where he put it on display at the Tennessee Exposition of 1897—right alongside another cabin said to be the original home of Lincoln's Confederate counterpart, Jefferson Davis. When questioned about the origins of the Lincoln cabin, Dennett's partner, evangelist James W. Bigham, explained (according to a reporter who was covering the exposition), "Lincoln was born in a log cabin, weren't he? Well, one cabin is as good as another."

After the exposition closed, Dennett disassembled the cabin and packed it away until 1901, when he again put it on display, this time at an exposition in Buffalo, New York. Eventually it wound up in the basement of a Long Island mansion. It was finally sold to a group of civic-minded preservationists, who turned it over to the federal government. Safely in the hands of the Interior Department, it was returned to Hodgenville, reassembled for the last time, and suitably installed in an elaborate memorial building.

In anticipation of questions about the cabin, the preservationists who donated it to the government undertook a major effort to dispel all doubts about it. They claimed to have collected "affidavits" from old settlers in the region who vouched for the cabin's authenticity. And they said the affidavits were "carefully reviewed" by a number of academic experts, including "Professors Hart of Harvard, Adams of Yale, and Turner of Wisconsin—officers of the American Historical Association—and Ida M. Tarbell, Lincoln's biographer.'" The experts, it was claimed, "agreed that the logs were genuine beyond a reasonable doubt."

Unfortunately none of the affidavits seem to have survived. Neither have the supporting statements made by the historians who had supposedly been consulted. Charles Hosmer, who has studied the controversy in depth, says there's no "conclusive proof that any of the distinguished professors ever declared the cabin authentic." It is hard to believe they ever would. All the contradictory evidence set aside, even partisans admitted the cabin had been moved, taken apart, and assembled half a dozen times or so. It is a little difficult to believe, therefore, that anyone could say with certainty that this cabin was *the* cabin.[4]

Another popular shrine is the home of Betsy Ross, located in Philadelphia. Yet there's no evidence she ever lived there. Both the U.S. Congress and the city of Philadelphia refused to accept the home as a gift because the claims of authenticity couldn't be verified. In 1949 the Joint State Government Commission of Pennsylvania concluded that "there is no proof that Betsy Ross lived here," although the commission acknowledged that "the house is an interesting example of the homes of the period."

The claim that Ross lived there was apparently advanced by the late-nineteenth-century owner of the house, perhaps in an attempt to increase its value. The house was scheduled to be destroyed in 1892, but at the last moment it was saved by preservationists, who had been encouraged in their efforts by a small-time painter who made money showing a picture of the building entitled "Birth of Our Nation's Flag."

Whether Ross ever lived in the house is a side issue at any

rate. Her chief claim to fame is that she invented the first American flag. Unfortunately, while it's possible she sewed the first flag, there's no evidence she designed it. What evidence there is concerning the origins of the flag suggests that one Francis Hopkinson deserves the credit. Records show that in May 1780 Hopkinson sent a bill to the Board of Admiralty for designing the "flag of the United States." Presumably Hopkinson could not have claimed credit for the flag if he hadn't been responsible for it since the people who knew the truth were still alive and could say otherwise.[5]

Claims that Stephen Foster wrote "My Old Kentucky Home" at Rowan Manor House near Bardstown, Kentucky, are as unfounded as the assertions made on behalf of the Betsy Ross home. Originally people were misled by a newspaper story published in the Louisville *Journal* in 1893. Later the myth was spread by promoters who bought the house with a public subscription and in 1922 donated the building to the state. Historians say that Foster composed the song in Pennsylvania, where he lived at the time.[6]

It may be that the average American doesn't care that the Lincoln, Ross, and Foster homes are fakes. Over the years Americans have shown an astonishing indifference to the relics of the past, fake or real. During the War of 1812 the room in which the Declaration of Independence was signed was slated for demolition and partly torn down. Preservationists managed to save the edifice, but only after two great wings of Independence Hall had already been destroyed. In 1853 a syndicate of enterprising Virginia businessmen attempted to turn Mount Vernon into a hotel. Appalled, the governor of Virginia sought to buy Washington's home, but when the owner demanded to be paid the going market rate of two hundred thousand dollars, the legislature refused to go along. Only the concentrated efforts of the Mount Vernon Ladies Association saved the building from commercial exploitation.

The homes of less famous patriots were not similarly spared. During the Civil War the John Hancock mansion was demolished so a developer could put to more profitable purposes the land underneath, which had grown in value to more than a hundred thousand dollars.[7]

Other shrines that have come under critical scrutiny are Henry Ford's Greenfield Village and John D. Rockefeller's better-known Colonial Williamsburg. Ford's paean to the "Early American Village" suffers from the sin of omission. Ford hated bankers, lawyers, socialites, and patricians, so in his ideal little town there aren't any. There are no banks, law offices, or mansions. Only comforting symbols of the past are allowed: an old windmill from Cape Cod; a New Hampshire farmhouse; Thomas Edison's Menlo Park laboratory.

Williamsburg, in its original form, was also incomplete. Although Rockefeller indicated he wanted everything to be accurate—"no scholar must ever be able to come to us and say we have made a mistake"—he left out any evidence that real people had ever lived there. His was a tidy world where mothers wore beautiful dresses and every family had a nice little home. To compound the inaccuracy, there were no slaves in his re-creation, not one, although more than 50 percent of the people in the real Williamsburg had been slaves. In the 1970's slaves were added. As one historian remarked, Williamsburg finally discovered slavery.[8]

Art

M any famous people whose appearances we think we know, we don't know at all. While almost everyone has seen pictures of Christopher Columbus, for instance, none is genuine. Not a single artist painted his picture during his lifetime.

John Harvard's appearance is also a mystery. The famous seated sculpture bearing his name in Harvard Yard is an utter invention. As was explained when the statue was unveiled in 1884, "There is not known to be extant a portrait or any delineation or description of his personality, his form, or features." The artist was congratulated for making Harvard appear scholarly and thoughtful. But for all we know, John Harvard might have looked like a well-fed beaver.

It's believed we have a better idea of what William Penn looked like, but no one can be sure. The only portrait of Penn with any credibility was painted not by an artist but by a druggist. Further, it was done from memory years after Penn had died, and paintings done posthumously are notoriously unreliable. Patrick Henry's portrait was painted sixteen years after he died by an artist who based the picture on a painting of Captain James Cook, whom Henry was said to resemble. Only later, when a genuine real-life miniature of Henry suddenly surfaced, was it discovered that Henry looked nothing like Cook.

For many years General Charles Lee, the disgraced Revolutionary War hero, was confused with one Arthur O'Connor, a foreigner. O'Connor's portrait, painted by Rembrandt Peale in 1803, was misidentified after 1845 as representing Lee. It wound up in numerous publications, including the *Cyclopedia of American Biography* and the *Magazine of American History*.

In the nineteenth century a booklet that purported to show the picture of each and every signer of the Declaration of Independence was circulated. Unfortunately twelve of the portraits, four of which hung in Independence Hall, were frauds. The images had been made up. No one knows what the men looked like.

What John Chapman (alias Johnny Appleseed) really looked like is also anybody's guess. The only picture in which he is said to appear is shrouded in mystery. It was supposedly drawn by a student at Oberlin College, but apparently no one knows by whom. To add to the confusion, in two books the figure in the drawing is dressed differently. In one he's wearing a long-peaked cap; in another, a big straw hat. More puzzlingly, he is pictured as carrying a pruning knife, although historian Dixon Wecter says he was known to believe it was "wicked" to prune trees.[1]

In another category are the artistic representations which were intentionally designed to put luminaries in a false and misleading light. Those of Daniel Boone, George Custer, and George Washington stand out.

Boone is remembered as a great Indian fighter and is so commemorated in Enrico Causici's marble figure above a door in the nation's Capitol rotunda, which shows him killing two Indians at the same time. The real Boone, however, merely tolerated Indian fighting and is said to have killed only one Indian his whole long life.[2]

Custer, despite his reputation as a loser, is depicted in innumerable paintings in romantic and idealistic hues. A typical example is a painting, reprinted in *The American Heritage History of the Indian Wars*, which memorializes his famous last stand. In the picture Custer, though battling bloodthirsty Indian savages, appears cool and in control. His brown army uniform is clean, neat, and perfectly buttoned. Custer himself, clean-shaven, sporting a neatly trimmed mustache, looks completely out of place, almost as if he has just been beamed into the battle from some remote and irenic scene. Even his hat is clean and perfectly angled.

How did he actually appear? Just as you'd expect a man to look after riding three hard days through dusty frontier territory: grimy, sweaty, and tired. His uniform was in tatters. His mustache was overgrown. His face covered with a full beard. In fact, he hadn't shaved in five weeks. As Custer scholar W. A. Graham points out, "He was far from being the natty, debonair, well-groomed cavalier of the pictures: he was a weary, dirty, unkempt man who, fighting desperately for life, had reached the limit of vitality and strength, and whose drawn and haggard features made him appear older than his age by many years."[3]

Thanks to artists' attempts to make him appear like a god, Washington's true image was usually grossly distorted. One bust of Washington was so idealized it actually lost its identity in the nineteenth century and for a time became known in the White House as the "Unknown Man." Horatio Greenough so mythologized Washington in a posthumous sculpture that contemporaries rebelled, refusing to place it in the Capitol, where it was originally intended to go. The statue features a half-naked Washington dressed in a toga, complete with sandals. Critics said it made Washington look ridiculous and indecent, and decency was "a subject on which he was known to be exceedingly fastidious."*

One biographer was so dissatisfied with the usual artists' renderings of Washington he had the publisher commission a new Washington portrait for the cover of his book.

What of the real Washington? What did he look like? As a

---

*One person was concerned the sculpture made Washington look impractical. "Washington was too prudent and careful of his health," he said, "to expose himself thus in a climate so uncertain as ours."

youth he had reddish brown hair—like Thomas Jefferson. As President he had gray hair, which he usually wore powdered. He did not regularly wear a wig. His complexion was sallow; his face, deeply pockmarked from smallpox contracted as a teenager. His chest was shallow; his shoulders were narrow; his arms and legs, like those of an old and long-retired athlete. Most surprising of all perhaps, he was tall—extremely tall by eighteenth-century standards—by some estimates six feet three, about the same as Lincoln. He wasn't dour-looking; the only reason we think he was is the Gilbert Stuart portraits, like the one reproduced on the dollar bill, which were painted when Washington was an old man. By then he had lost most of his teeth and had to make do with his famous ill-fitting dentures. Stuart tried to remedy the problem by stuffing cotton padding into Washington's mouth to restore his original facial expression, but with less than great success.[4]

The invention of photography diminished the visual misrepresentation of great men but did not altogether eliminate the problem. This is evident from any number of photos of political figures. Of these, one of the most notorious shows Calvin Coolidge dressed like a farmer with a shovel in his hand. Coolidge wasn't much of a farmer, of course, but then, probably few people were fooled by the picture. In the background of the photograph, taken somewhere in a field, a Secret Service agent, dressed in a suit, leaning against a shiny new car, can be seen. Coolidge himself is wearing shiny shoes fit for the office.

Less well known but just as delightful is a publicity photo which shows Robert Moses, the architect of New York State's highway system, behind the wheel of a car as he pays a toll at one of his bridges. As Moses's biographer Robert Caro points out, the photograph is doubly wrong. Moses never paid tolls at any of his bridges, and though he designed all the major roadways in New York City, including the Long Island Expressway, he never personally drove on any of them. He was always driven by a chauffeur. The man who single-handedly was responsible for building billions of dollars in new highways—more highways than anybody else in history—never learned how to drive.[5]

Photographs do show us what great men look like—but not always accurately. For people who care about such things, the mole on Lincoln's face appeared on his right cheek, though it frequently can be seen on the left because the photo has been reversed. Usually this happens by mistake, but in the nineteenth century it occurred by design. When Lincoln ran for President in 1860, there were so few full-length portraits available that publishers arranged to put Lincoln's head on other people's bodies; if the head needed to be reversed to fit the existing portrait, it was. Stefan Lorant reports that Lincoln's head found its way onto the bodies of Henry Clay, Andrew Jackson, John C. Frémont, and even little Martin Van Buren. One publisher had the gall to put Lincoln's head on the body of states' rights advocate John C. Calhoun—though the publisher did have the good taste to alter the inscriptions on several papers in the background which supported the southern cause. The slogan on one document, "The Sovereignty of the States," was delicately changed to read "Proclamation of Freedom."

The practice of changing the heads of people's bodies was widespread. It's not known if anybody ever complained.[6]

Just as interesting as the misrepresentation of famous people in photographs and art has been the distortion of significant events related to war, particularly the Revolutionary War. The first famous picture to come out of the Revolution, Paul Revere's print of the Boston Massacre, was riddled with errors—all deliberately made. Revere shows the British troops firing at once; Hiller Zobel, author of a book on the massacre, says the muskets actually "banged almost at will" in a disorganized fashion. Revere has British Captain Thomas Preston, sword raised in command, egging his troops on; Zobel says Preston never ordered his troops to fire and was utterly surprised when they did.

Revere's print is a masterful work of propaganda, with good and evil clearly delineated. In the background, on the British side of the picture, is a building labeled "Butcher's Hall." On the colonists' side there's a quaint half-moon and even a little dog. The colonists, of course, are unarmed, though Revere undoubtedly knew the incident began when a British soldier was hit with a thrown club.[7]

The Battle of Lexington, the first battle of the Revolution, has been the subject of an increasingly distorted series of pictures. When it was first portrayed by Doolittle and Earle in 1775, it looked like a tiny, insignificant encounter, hardly a battle at all, which is about how historians describe it. If anybody comes off well, it's the British, who are lined up in impressive columns, twenty or thirty soldiers wide. The American minutemen, in contrast, scattering this way and that, hardly look as if they even wanted to fight. In a second picture, done in 1830 by Pendleton, the minutemen put up a bit more of a fight, but the bulk of the men still seem to be running off. Only nine, seven firing, two loading, courageously face the enemy. By 1855, in a print by an artist named Billings, the minutemen are doing much better. Only a few have dispersed, and as many as eighteen are loading and firing their weapons. Standing shoulder to shoulder, they appear to be giving the British a hell of a fight.

Their best effort was yet to come. In a mural done in 1886 for the Lexington town hall, the minutemen, each and every one of them, can be seen resisting the onslaught of the British in the face of overwhelming odds. As described by Stewart Holbrook, "There is no dispersing, not even a shadow of wavering. *Here* is battle. The patriot line holds from end to end, like a stone fence. Some of the Minutemen are dying, but all others are either loading or firing—emptying their muskets into the glittering target offered by the British light infantry. . . . Let them who will, write a nation's history. Give me the boys who draw the pictures."[8]

Two other pictures from the Revolution deserve mention. Both involve Washington: praying at Valley Forge and crossing the Delaware.

Notwithstanding all the pictures that show Washington kneeling at prayer in the deep snow at Valley Forge, an image of which was reprinted on a postage stamp in 1928 and cast in bronze on the wall of the Sub-Treasury Building in New York City, there's no evidence he ever did so. Artists got the story from Parson Weems, the same Parson Weems who invented the cherry tree story. Weems says he got it from a Quaker named Potts, "if I mistake not."[9]

Washington did indeed cross the Delaware, but not in the dramatic and elegant style depicted in Emanuel Leutze's famous painting. Washington probably wasn't standing, of course; that would have been, as one writer plainly put it, "stupid." And Washington probably wasn't quite as impassive as Leutze portrays him. (One is reminded of all those pictures which show Washington quietly atop his horse with bullets whirring speedily around him. As one critic commented, at times his horses seem more active than the general himself.) Furthermore, the American flag probably wasn't flying; while the flag was in existence at this time, it hadn't yet been adopted by Congress. Finally, Washington's boat probably wasn't filled to capacity; there wouldn't have been any need for crowding. Boats there were aplenty; it was men who were in short supply.[10]

Whether it's accurate or not, virtually everybody is under the impression that the painting, which was done in the 1850's, was designed to stir up patriotic American feelings, but that may not be true either. Historian Ann Hawkes Hutton contends that Leutze, a German, painted the picture primarily to stir up Germans. Leutze, she says, hoped that by celebrating the American Revolution, he could help bring about revolution in Germany, where he painted the picture. Leutze reportedly hoped that just as the famous Delaware crossing had rallied Americans to the cause of the revolution, so his painting would encourage Germans to rebel against the conservative governments that had recently crushed the Revolution of 1848. It didn't, however.[11]

Among other historic paintings, one of the most interesting is Thomas Hill's renowned rendition of the golden spike ceremony, which celebrated the joining of the Union Pacific and Central Pacific railroads in Utah in 1869. Hill's painting gives the impression that the ceremony was like a small-town nineteenth-century

Fourth of July picnic. The painting shows men in frock coats, women in long, elegant dresses, and in the background, waving in the wind, several broad, clean American flags.

The real spirit of the occasion was captured in a photograph by Colonel Charles Savage. Not only are most of the people in the crowd wearing work clothes; but several are holding liquor bottles, and many are evidently drunk. There are even a few "painted" women, said by historians to be work camp prostitutes.[12]

One final myth perpetrated by artists involves housing, not heroes. Many Americans firmly believe the Pilgrims lived in log cabins. They didn't. The Pilgrims probably didn't even know what a log cabin looked like. Log cabins had been virtually unknown in England and weren't built in America until late in the seventeenth century, when they were introduced by Germans and Swedes. Not even the settlers at Jamestown lived in log cabins. The very term "log cabin" can't even be found in print before the 1770's.[13]

The Good
Old Days

The vague feeling that things are bad and getting worse is only partly due to the fact that certain things *are* getting worse. Much of the despair really stems from the erroneous belief that many of our problems are new.

Crime is particularly thought of as a modern problem. Yet authorities say crime was considered a major social question a hundred years ago. Crime was so feared that the Charleston *News and Chronicle* reported: "Murder and violence are the distinguishing marks of our civilization." Another journal wrote: "Each day we see ghastly records of crime . . . murder seems to have run riot and each citizen asks . . . 'Who is safe?'" The journal which raised this issue was not the New York *Post* or the *Daily News* in the 1980's, but *Leslie's Weekly* in 1868. Statistics indicate that people had reason to be afraid. One expert has estimated that the crime rate between 1860 and 1890 rose more than twice as fast as the population.

One of the most popular current complaints is that the courts have tilted the justice system so far in favor of the defendants that no one is safe anymore. The assumption, of course, is that there existed a period when the courts were tough on criminals, a time when the sheriff got his man and the courts put the man away. Perhaps there was such a time, but when? In William Howard Taft's day? Taft grumbled that the law so favored the criminal that trials seemed "like a game of chance." Twenty years later Herbert Hoover complained that everybody "knows full well" that "procedures unduly favor the criminal." In a statement that could have come from any politician alive today, he said, "In our desire to be merciful the pendulum has swung in favor of the prisoner and far away from protection of society." In the 1930's the Wickersham and Seabury investigations concluded, in the words of Bergen Evans, "that a criminal had about a ninety-nine-per-cent chance of escaping punishment." Well before the Warren Court, the Chicago Crime Commission estimated that "approximately ninety-seven percent of the burglaries and ninety-one percent of the robberies committed in Chicago in 1951 did not even result in an indictment for the offense committed." And as Evans points out, "an indictment is a long way from a conviction, and a conviction is sometimes a long way from serving a sentence." Cold-blooded hired guns, who killed for money, had even less worry of being put away. Of some seven hundred paid assassinations in Chicago between the 1930's and the early 1950's, there were fewer than ten convictions.

Other mistaken notions involving crime are that fewer people seem to go to jail now than at the beginning of the century, that justice suffers because of plea bargaining, that most people who are arrested for serious crimes manage to get off scot-free.

The first of these canards is easily disproved by statistics, which clearly indicate that proportionately more convicted felons are sent to jail now than sixty years ago when, as historian Charles Silberman has pointed out, "the accused had far fewer protections."

The belief that the justice system has been undermined in modern times by plea bargaining is based on the erroneous assumption that it is a recent innovation. In fact, as Silberman reports, "it has been the dominant means of settling criminal cases for the last century." As for the belief that plea bargaining is being used by hard-pressed prosecutors to save time, evidence suggests it's about as prevalent in slow rural courts as in crowded urban ones. Defenders of the practice, like Silberman, say it is being used everywhere for the very simple reason that it is a just way of making "the punishment fit the crime."

That arrested offenders usually go free is simply untrue. It's not even true in New York City. One respected study has shown that 88 percent of the suspects arrested for robbery there in recent years were convicted. Most were sentenced to jail.[1]

Poverty is another one of those problems which have longer histories than most people imagine. Critics began noticing poverty on a large scale in the United States as long ago as the early 1800's. Observations about the paradox of poverty, the belief that poverty is out of place in a country as rich as ours, were first made in 1822. "Our territory is so expansive, its soil so prolific," said the Society for the Prevention of Pauperism in that year, that poverty should be "foreign to our country."[2]

If anything, poverty is less of a problem now than it used to be. Nothing we have today compares with the horrible conditions of tenement life common in the Gilded Age, when it was not unusual for a poor family of eight to share a living room measuring ten feet by twelve feet and a bedroom six feet by eight feet. Poverty then was so widespread it is estimated *half* the population of New York City lived in slums. Today people are worried because twenty thousand New Yorkers are homeless; in 1884 more than forty-three thousand families in New York City were evicted from their homes because they couldn't make the rent.[3]

Things weren't much better in the 1920's. While a lot of people prospered, most were poor. Frederick Lewis Allen points out that according to a famous study by the Brookings Institution, 60 percent of American families in the golden year of 1929 earned less than the amount considered necessary to meet basic human needs: two thousand dollars a year. Worse, 40 percent lived on less than fifteen hundred dollars a year. In the farm states the situation was even worse. In Muncie, Indiana, in 1924, between 70 and 88 percent of the families earned annually less than the requisite two thousand dollars. In Zanesville, Ohio, in 1926, 70 percent lived below the poverty line.

Since the 1920's, poverty has declined dramatically. To judge by one study, which took into account the minimum standards of decency established by the government at the respective times in question, the poverty rate fell from 33 percent in 1940 to 27 percent in 1950 to 21 percent in 1960 to 11 percent in 1970. Thus it appears that concern about poverty rose as the problem itself declined. Put another way, all that increased over the years was the Americans' consciousness of the problem—in itself a positive development.[4]

At the same time that poverty was declining, the quality of life for most Americans was rising. Historian Ruth Cowan has pointed out that in 1940 "one out of three Americans was still carrying water in buckets, and two out of three Americans did not enjoy the comforts of central heating." In 1980 only one million housing units out of eighty-seven million nationwide lacked running water; only three million did not have a complete bathroom. Furthermore, in 1980 only sixteen million households made do without central heating, "and the vast majority of those were in parts of the country where such comforts were not necessary."[5]

It may be thought, however, that while we have made progress in one area or another, overall we're worse off than we used to be. But the fact is many of the most characteristic troubles of recent times—high unemployment, instability, bankruptcy—mirror troubles common in the past. Even excluding the Great Depression, one can point to panics and depressions in 1837, 1873, and 1893 that were just as severe as anything suffered in the 1970's. One expert has calculated that there were recessions in fourteen of the last twenty-five years of the nineteenth century. During that period entrepreneurs learned to accept failure as part of the American way of life. It's been estimated that 95 percent of the entrepreneurs in business at that time failed. Contrary to popular impression, the people who failed didn't take their setbacks in stride. Even John D. Rockefeller himself later wondered how "we came through them. You know how often I had not an unbroken night's sleep, worrying about how it was all coming out. All the fortune I have made has not served to compensate for the anxiety of that period. Work by day and worry by night, week in and week out, month after month."

The pessimists who spoke knowingly about the plight of the country in the 1970's frequently mentioned in particular the energy crisis, as if that in itself marked a turning point of some kind. Even historians, who should have known better, warned that the country was entering an unprecedented era of decline and limits. Writing in *The New York Times*, Harvard historian David Donald said economic circumstances had so changed that American history had become virtually irrelevant. He indicated it would almost be foolish to continue teaching American history since the country's history taught the lesson of abundance, and now abundance there was no more. In the coming school term, he said, his main goal would be to disenthrall his students "from the spell of history, to help them see the irrelevance of the past, to assist them in understanding what Lincoln meant in saying, 'The dogmas of the quiet past are inadequate to the stormy present.'"

Upon analysis, the only thing in dangerously short supply in the seventies may have been historical perspective. As we now know, the energy crisis wasn't as bad as it seemed. Oil eventually flowed again, Americans learned to conserve, and the inflation rate was cut. Most important of all, Americans proved they could adapt to changing circumstances—just as they had in the past.[6]

Pollution is another of the great modern problems that aren't really quite so modern as we think. Nothing may match the possibly fatal consequences of the pollution at Love Canal or the dangers of acid rain, but pollution was so bad in some early industrial communities that the towns had to pick up and move to escape it. One visitor to Chicago in the late 1800's commented that the pollution was so stifling that during his one week's stay he "did not

Legends, Lies, and Cherished Myths

see in Chicago anything but darkness, smoke, [or] clouds of dirt."

In several important ways, pollution today is less of a problem than it was a hundred years ago. New York in the late nineteenth century was so polluted one critic called it a "nasal disaster." Sewers were often clogged, garbage was strewn about, and pigs freely roamed the streets. (In some cities there were more pigs than people.) Worst of all was the pollution produced by horses. At the turn of the century New Yorkers owned 150,000 horses, each of which produced as much as twenty-five pounds of manure a day— enough to turn even the most fashionable addresses into stink holes.[7]

That America used to be a more secure place is widely believed but is only partly true. From the end of the War of 1812 until World War II Americans didn't have to worry about foreign attacks. But earlier they frequently did live in daily fear of outside aggression. In colonial times, as David Hackett Fischer observes, American life was punctuated by the recurrent cry of war. "From the beginnings of settlement to 1815," he reports, "there was a war in every American generation, and some of these wars were cruel and bloody. It is unlikely that a civilized society, anywhere in the world, has ever survived losses in proportion to those Virginia experienced in its first half century." New England's history was hardly better. In the little-known King Philip's War (1675–76), thousands were killed, more than half a dozen thriving communities were destroyed or abandoned, and several towns suffered extensive arson. Relative to population, the war caused more casualties than either Germany or Russia suffered during World War II. "The Anglo-American population, of course, was very much smaller than these great nations," Fischer acknowledges, "but the social impact must have been comparable." In hard numbers, one in every twenty-two Russians was a casualty in World War II; one in every twenty New Englanders was injured or killed in King Philip's War.[8]

Of all of today's social problems, none seems more modern than drug abuse. Yet even drug abuse was widespread a hundred years ago. If we leave aside the millions addicted to alcohol, it's estimated there were a hundred thousand drug addicts in America in the late 1860's. One doctor in Ohio insisted that in his town there were more addicts than alcoholics. Cincinnati was said to be so menaced by drug addicts that you could meet opium slaves by the score on almost any street. "They are slaves, abject slaves suffering exquisite torture," reported a contemporary. "Once in the fetters of opium and morphia, they are, with few exceptions, fettered for life."[9]

It would be as foolish to think that things are always getting better as it is to assume they're steadily worsening. The amazing development is that we now have to be on our guard against undue pessimism. Through much of our history the problem has been excessive and mindless optimism.

Folklore

Many of the most famous figures in American folklore believed to be mythical were actually real, but hardly anybody seems prepared to believe it. It has been pointed out repeatedly that there was a real railroad engineer named Casey Jones who, at the turn of the century, did indeed courageously sacrifice his own life to save the lives of his passengers. But ever since the ballad about him became part of the national folklore shortly after his death, he has seemed, and seems destined to remain, a creature of fiction. John Henry has also been identified in numerous scholarly works as a real black railroad worker, and in 1940 he was even the subject of a play starring Paul Robeson specifically designed "to disinter him for the Broadway stage." But all anyone recalls is the legend about a fictional man who died trying to beat a steam drill, a story that may or may not be true. The fact that the story was based on a real-life figure of formidable physical powers is forgotten.[1]

Mrs. O'Leary probably wished sometimes that she were just a fictional character and that the Chicago fire were a figment of someone's imagination. But she actually lived, she actually had a cow, and the fire that burned down much of Chicago in 1871 actually started in her barn. All that is unknown is how the fire started. Some newspapers at the time blamed the cow, which was accused of kicking over a lantern because it supposedly hadn't been milked. Others blamed Mrs. O'Leary, who was said to have started the fire in anger because her relief payments had been cut off. Unfortunately for this explanation, there is no evidence she was angry, her payments hadn't been cut off—and she wasn't on relief. All that is known for sure is that the fire started at the barn behind her house at 137 De Koven Street.[2]

John Chapman, aka Johnny Appleseed, not only lived, he really did tramp through the Ohio Valley planting trees. But he wasn't poor, he wasn't a hermit, and he didn't, as alleged in one folktale, plant seeds on the grave of a sweetheart in such a way that when they matured, they spelled the phrase "Apple Blossoms." According to historian Richard Dorson, Johnny was basically a well-liked nurseryman whose chief "contribution lay in moving his nurseries west to keep abreast of the receding frontier." He may very well have liked to walk barefoot, but the fact is he probably didn't need to; he was so successful that by the end of his life he had accumulated more than twelve hundred acres of land. As for his general appearance, nothing is known for sure. But by one account, given credence by Dorson, he dressed just about like everybody else on the frontier, down to Indian moccasins on his feet.[3]

Uncle Sam was a real person, too, by the name of Sam Wilson and, as fate would have it, one of Johnny Appleseed's boyhood friends. Wilson didn't wear striped pants and didn't have a long white beard. But he did wear a top hat and in his own day became a symbol of the United States government. The identification with the government came during the War of 1812, when Wilson began supplying meat to troops stationed around Troy, New York. Meat sent to the soldiers was stamped "U.S." for United States. But when a government inspector came along to check on the meat, he was told by an imaginative worker in Wilson's store that the initials stood for "Uncle Sam," Wilson's nickname. Soon all federal supplies were said to belong to "Uncle Sam."

For many years scholars discounted claims that Uncle Sam had been named in honor of Sam Wilson, but in 1961 a scholar discovered an 1830 newspaper which gave credence to the story. The newspaper quoted a soldier from the War of 1812 who claimed to have been at Wilson's store the day the inspector was told about the initials. In the early 1960's the U.S. Congress officially proclaimed Wilson the original Uncle Sam.[4]

Just as there are real people falsely believed to be mythical, so there are mythical figures falsely thought to be real. Among these is Mother Goose. In her case, belief was seemingly substantiated by a wealth of detail. It was said that Mother Goose was actually Elizabeth (Foster) Goose, that she was born in Boston in 1665, that she married Isaac Goose at age twenty-seven, and that she reared sixteen children, six her own and ten her husband's. Adding to the realism was the claim that her songs were published by a characteristically spiteful son-in-law, Thomas Fleet, with an unflattering picture of an openmouthed, gooselike creature on the title page.

As it turns out, there really was an Elizabeth Goose, but she had nothing to do with the famous nursery rhymes; the Mother Goose rhymes were the work of Charles Perrault, the same Frenchman who invented the tales of Cinderella and Sleeping Beauty.

Perrault didn't coin the term "Mother Goose," but it was his book, *Tales of My Mother Goose*, published in 1696–97, which apparently popularized the phrase, first in France, then, in 1777, in translation in Britain. The story linking Elizabeth Goose to Mother Goose, in contrast, didn't come about until the mid-nineteenth century, when one of her descendants claimed in a magazine article that her songs had been published in a book printed in 1719. The book, alas, can't be found; scholars say it never existed.[5]

Paul Bunyan wasn't a real person, and no one thinks he was; but most people are under the mistaken impression he was a creation of folklore. In fact, he is one of the prime examples of what Dorson has called "fakelore"—an ersatz creation developed to meet the American need for instant homegrown folk heroes. While he is said to have "a trickle of oral tradition" behind him, the basic facts about Bunyan were made up out of the blue by writers and advertisers—not by plain folks and not a long time ago either. A hundred years ago no one had ever heard of Paul Bunyan.

The story which made Bunyan famous, in fact, was created by an advertising man, W. B. Laughead, in the 1920's for the purpose of selling products for the Red River Lumber Company. As such, Paul is about as authentic a folk hero as Mr. Clean or the Jolly Green Giant—that is to say, not very authentic at all, unless it be held that folklore can emanate from an elite, a birth that doesn't seem logical. Laughead himself confessed that when he created the Bunyan stories, all he had in mind was selling lumber. "We were not thinking of the Paul Bunyan material as literature," he later acknowledged, "but merely as a vehicle for advertising." A sample suggests he was telling the truth. In one story, published in 1922, Bunyan and friends come across like accountants at a budget hearing. "Babe, the big blue ox," is said to constitute "Paul Bunyan's assets and liabilities." When cost sheets are figured on Babe, Johnny Inkslinger discovers that "upkeep and overhead" are "expensive but the charges for operation and depreciation" are "low and the efficiency" is very high.[6]

Of all our folk heroes, Santa Claus is probably the most familiar and the most misunderstood. To begin with, the name is strictly an Americanism; in Europe he was known for centuries as St. Nicholas. The change occurred when the Dutch, spelling his name "Sint Nikolass," imported Nicholas to America. Somewhere along the way the name became "Sinterklass" and finally "Santa Claus."

More surprising, Santa Claus didn't always arrive at Christmas. In Europe he showed up on December 6, as he did in the early years in America. He became specifically associated with Christmas only when Americans of British ancestry adopted him from the Dutch.

Most interesting of all, Santa Claus didn't always look the way he does now. The Dutch made him out to look like Fred Astaire, thin, tall, and dignified. Later, in the early 1800's, Washington Irving imagined Santa as a bulky man who smoked a pipe and wore baggy pants. In a drawing in *Harper's Weekly* in 1858 he doesn't even have a beard. Not until the Civil War did he begin to look the way we think he should, thanks to a cartoon drawn by Thomas Nast.

Santa hasn't changed much since then, but he got Rudolph, the red-nosed reindeer, only in 1939, when Montgomery Ward came up with the idea.[7]

Famous Quotes

Quotations often aren't remembered; they're misremembered. They are subject to myriad errors. If the quotation is not mangled, it is misattributed. If by chance it is properly attributed, it still may be misinterpreted. If it is really famous, it is apt to be all three: mangled, misattributed, and misinterpreted.

We probably shouldn't call them famous quotes. Famous misquotes would be better.

"The Pursuit of Happiness"

The famous phrase from the Declaration of Independence about every American's right to life, liberty, and the pursuit of happiness is nearly universally revered, endlessly repeated, and barely understood. The problem is with the words "pursuit of happiness." Grade school teachers speak of the pursuit of happiness in the same way one would speak of a person pursuing a dream. Actually, in Jefferson's day the word "pursuit" had a far more practical meaning. It was then used in the same way we use the word when talking about someone's pursuing a career; no one in the eighteenth century used it to mean a quest. As Arthur Schlesinger observed, it is thus the peoples' right not just to strive for happiness but to obtain it. The Declaration itself makes this clear in a reference to the government's duty to the people to "effect their safety and happiness." Even conservatives like John Adams agreed, Adams himself saying in one place that "the happiness of society is the end of government."[1]

"The Mass of Mankind Has Not Been Born with Saddles on their Backs"

Jefferson said it, but he did not originate the line that "the mass of mankind has not been born with saddles on their backs, nor a favored few booted and spurred, ready to ride them legitimately by the grace of God." Jefferson evidently lifted the statement almost verbatim from a speech made by Richard Rumbold, the seventeenth-century English politician. According to a book published in 1734 (before Jefferson was born), Rumbold remarked in a famous speech that he "did not believe that God had made the greater part of mankind with saddles on their backs, and bridles in their mouths, and some few booted and spurred to ride the rest."[2]

"One Life to Lose for My Country"

Young and courageous he was, but when he died, Nathan Hale did not say, "I only regret that I have but one life to lose for my country." At least that's not what he said according to Captain Frederick Mackenzie, a British officer who witnessed Hale's death.

Mackenzie's recently discovered diary states that Hale's last words were: "It is the duty of every good officer to obey any orders given him by his commander-in-chief."[3]

"In the Name of the Great Jehovah and the Continental Congress"

According to one historian, not only did Ethan Allen not demand the surrender of Fort Ticonderoga in 1775 "in the name of the great Jehovah and the Continental Congress!," he didn't have the right to. "In truth," according to Professor Van Tyne, "he had no commission from either of those high authorities." In fact, Benedict Arnold was the only American on the expedition who held an actual commission from the Continental Congress.

It was Allen himself who claimed—four years later—to have uttered the famous phrase. Others, however, remembered his saying something more colloquial, such as "Come out of there, you damned old rat." The British commander later said Allen never mentioned either the great Jehovah or the Continental Congress: "[He] told me his orders were from the province of Connecticut."[4]

"Your People Are a Great Beast"

Naked Hamilton baiting may be responsible for the belief that Alexander Hamilton so utterly distrusted the masses that he once cried out, "Your people are a great beast." The quotation was attributed to Hamilton by Henry Adams, the descendant of one of his enemies, on the dubious authority of Theophilus Parsons, another Hamilton foe. Parsons said he'd heard it from a friend who in turn was relating a story *he* had once heard. The statement was supposedly made at a dinner held shortly after the adoption of the Constitution, but it was never corroborated by anyone else and wasn't published until 1859, long after Hamilton died.

Whether Hamilton said it or not may not matter much anyway. Hamilton's suspicions about "the people" are well known and hardly need further substantiation. If anything, Adams's use of the dubious quotation may tell us more about him than about Hamilton.[5]

"Millions for Defense"

Even in his own lifetime Charles C. Pinckney vigorously denied saying, "Millions for defense, but not once cent for tribute." What he actually said, after French Foreign Minister Talleyrand demanded a $250,000 bribe to open peace talks with the United States was: "No, no, not a sixpence."

The "millions for defense" quip originated with Robert Goodloe Harper, a prominent South Carolina legislator. According to a report in the *American Daily Advertiser*, dated June 20, 1798, Harper used the line in making a toast to John Marshall, one of the envoys sent over to France to help Pinckney negotiate with the French. The toast was made in the course of a dinner given by Congress in Marshall's honor.[6]

"I Do Not Know Much About the Tariff"

Lincoln is held in such high regard almost everybody wants him on their side. That accounts for the attempt to attribute the following bogus protariff statement to him: "I do not know much about the tariff, but I know this much, when we buy manufactured goods abroad, we get the goods and the manufacturer gets the money. When we buy manufactured goods at home, we get both the goods and the money. When an American paid $20 for steel rails to an English manufacturer, America had the steel and England the $20. But when he paid $20 for the steel to an American manufacturer, America had both the steel and the $20."

Lincoln didn't say it because he couldn't have said it. He died two weeks before the first rails were ever rolled in this country.[7]

"God Must Have Loved the Common People"

Lincoln probably would have liked to say, "God must have loved the common people; he made so many of them," but it's proved he didn't. The phrase was actually made up by James Morgan in a 1928 book entitled *Our Presidents*. As it happens, Morgan himself has not even been quoted properly. In Morgan's account, Lincoln says, "Friend, the Lord prefers common-looking people. That is the reason he makes so many of them." (According to Morgan, the expression came to Lincoln during a dream in which someone in a crowd remarked that Lincoln "is a very common-looking man.")[8]

"You Can Fool All the People"

It may be true that "You can fool all the people some of the time and some of the people all of the time, but you cannot fool all the people all the time," but Lincoln probably didn't say it. He was supposed to have made the remark on September 8, 1858, in Clinton, Illinois, when he was running for the Senate against Stephen Douglas, but the local papers made no mention of it. A few people who claimed to have heard the speech said he said something like it—but they said that only some fifty years after the speech was given, in response to an inquiry by the Chicago *Tribune* and the Brooklyn *Eagle*.[9]

"Of the People"

Lincoln said it at Gettysburg: "Government of the people, by the people, for the people." But the remark has been traced to at least two speeches given earlier by other public figures. Theodore Parker, a Unitarian minister and abolitionist, said: "[G]overnment becomes more and more of all, by all and for all." And Daniel Webster talked about "The people's government, made for the people, made by the people, and answerable to the people."[10]

"If I Knew What Brand He Used, I'd Send Every General a Barrel"

Lincoln never said, in response to complaints about Grant's drinking, "If I knew what brand he used, I'd send every other general in the field a barrel of it." The quip was made up by Charles Halpine for a fictional story about a banquet. Lincoln himself not only denied saying it but added that it sounded like the old anecdote told about England's George II. When people complained that General James Wolfe was mad, the king allegedly said, "If General Wolfe is mad, I hope he bites some of my other generals."

At any rate, Grant's drinking didn't need defending. While he drank a lot when he was unemployed in Illinois, after he joined the Army, he was never drunk.[11]

"Go West, Young Man, Go West"

Horace Greeley is glued to the phrase "Go west, young man, go west," but whether he should be is a matter of terrific confusion. Even traditionalists who insist he said it can't agree when he said it. Biographer Henry Luther Stoddard says he first said it as early as 1837. The author of a recent book of quotations says Greeley wrote it in *Hints Toward Reform* in 1850. Biographer William Harlan Hale says that "no one" knows when he first said it but insists "all America" knew Greeley did say it first and cites an 1854 letter in which Greeley used the expression. "The truth of the matter," says Hale, "was that Greeley had either said it or written it in substance to hundreds of people who had come to him for advice."

Greeley credited the quotation himself, however, according to *Bartlett's*, to John Babson Lane Soule, a little-known Indiana journalist, who is said to have "first" used it in 1851 in the Terre Haute *Express*.[12]

"Cross of Gold"

It's popularly thought that the long career of William Jennings Bryan was launched in 1896, when he brought down the National Democratic Convention with his famous warning to advocates of the gold standard: "You shall not press down upon the brow of labor this crown of thorns. You shall not crucify mankind upon a cross of gold." Some even seem convinced no one had ever heard of the Nebraska orator before this speech. Republicans in the East sneered that Bryan was nothing more than an ignorant upstart.

Bryan actually was already famous. By 1896 he was regarded as the master orator of the Democratic party. A two-term congressman, he had won national recognition for his speeches on the House floor. When Bryan got up to give his cross of gold address, delegates, eager to hear the reputed spellbinder of the West, crowded into the convention hall.

The claim has been made that the speech was so well delivered and so powerful that it won Bryan the party's presidential nomination. But this isn't true either. By the time he gave the speech, Bryan had carefully lined up so many delegates to vote for him that his nomination was assured. The speech merely marked the climax of his efforts to win the nomination, not the beginning.[13]

"Perdicaris Alive or Raisuli Dead!"

That Teddy Roosevelt said this in an effort to free Perdicaris from the hands of his Moroccan kidnapper Raisuli is probably believed because it sounds so like him. In truth the expression was coined by a pithy wire service reporter, Edwin M. Hood of the Associated Press, after reading a message the secretary of state was preparing to send to Morocco. The secretary instantly adopted it in the government's official message. Roosevelt subsequently included it in a political message *he* sent to the GOP convention then meeting in Chicago to nominate himself as President.[14]

"Lafayette, We Are Here"

That an American uttered this inspired remark when American troops entered Paris in 1917 is true as everyone believes. But nice as it might have been for General Pershing to have said it, alas, he didn't. Pershing wasn't much of a speaker, so he appointed Colonel Charles E. Stanton to deliver the official speech. It was Stanton who had the genius to say, "Lafayette, we are here."[15]

"Promises Are Like Pie Crusts—Made to Be Broken"

This is one of those quotations that survive and flourish because they are so serviceable. Attributed to Vladimir Lenin, it is said to prove the Soviets can't be trusted. Why, they themselves admit it!

Whether they can or can't be trusted is an interesting question, but this quotation can't be any help in determining the answer. Morris Kominsky, who tracked down the quotation with the help of the Library of Congress, says it's been completely misunderstood. It can be found in Lenin's published works, but it appears in the course of a bitter denunciation of socialist colleagues who wrongly believed, said Lenin, that promises are made to be broken.[16]

"Fall Like an Overripe Fruit into Our Hands"

Another quotation frequently attributed to Lenin—that America would fall one day "like an overripe fruit into our hands"—is also bogus. There is no known source for the quotation, and authorities in the field, according to the Library of Congress, doubt Lenin ever made the statement because he was almost "wholly uninterested in the United States (his interest lay in the hope of a Communist revolution in Europe)."[17]

"The Only Thing We Have to Fear"

The claim "The only thing we have to fear is fear itself" is identified with Franklin Roosevelt, but remarks with a similar ring have been made by several other equally famous people. One person even traced the quote to the Bible, which says, "Be not afraid of sudden fear." Closer to FDR's formulation was Montaigne's "The thing I fear most is fear." But one shouldn't overlook Francis Bacon's "Nothing is terrible except fear itself." Also worth remembering: Wellington's "The only thing I am afraid of is fear" and Thoreau's "Nothing is so much to be feared as fear."[18]

"When the United States Gets Fascism"

It's apparently true that Huey Long said something like "When the United States gets fascism, it will call it anti-fascism." But the person to whom he allegedly made the statement, writer Robert Cantwell, says that Long never used those words precisely. Arthur Schlesinger, Jr. has indicated his doubts about the authenticity of the quotation, concluding it was a little too intellectual for Long.[19]

"Even if 300,000,000 Chinese Were Killed in an Atomic War"

When the statement "Even if 300,000,000 Chinese were killed in an atomic war, there would still remain 300,000,000" first appeared, it was attributed to "Chinese leaders." Later it was attributed to Mao Zedong, who, in view of his reputation, surely seemed a likely choice. But the United States State Department has said it was probably uttered by Marshal Peng Teh-huai. The government says there's no evidence Mao ever "officially expressed this viewpoint."[20]

Acknowledgments

Most of the people who helped me with this book don't realize they did. I want to thank them anyway. So here's to all the scholars who have churned out the little-read but useful articles and books cited in my notes on sources. Without their diligent efforts, this book never would have been possible.

I am immensely indebted to Bernard Weisberger for catching many of the kinds of errors in my manuscript which I have pointed out in other writers' works.

Also of assistance, particularly in helping me say what I meant to say, were Stephen McAdoo, Rod Decker, and Michael Reed.

Of all the people who need to be acknowledged, Mike Youngren deserves to be acknowledged most, for allowing me time off from my job as a reporter so I could complete this book.

As always, editor Howard Cady provided me with the kind of help editors supposedly don't provide anymore.

Notes

Discoverers and Inventors

1. Washington Irving, *The Life and Voyages of Christopher Columbus* (1828; rpt. Twayne Publishers, 1981), pp. 47–53; Samuel Eliot Morison, *Admiral of the Ocean Sea* (1942), vol. I, p. 117; Samuel Eliot Morison, *The European Discovery of America: The Northern Voyages* (1971), p. 6; Harvey Einbinder, *The Myth of the Britannica* (1964), pp. 169–72.

2. Morison, *Admiral of the Ocean Sea*, vol. I, pp. 137–38.

3. Morison, *European Discovery of America: The Northern Voyages*, ch. 3; Emily Morison Beck, ed., *Sailor Historian: The Best of Samuel Eliot Morison* (1977), pp. 17–18.

4. Morison, *Admiral of the Ocean Sea*, vol. II, p. 271. S. E. Ackerman, *Popular Fallacies* (1924), pp. 603–06.

5. Howard Zinn, *A People's History of the United States* (1980), pp. 1–8.

6. Frederick J. Pohl, *Amerigo Vespucci* (1944), p. 63 ff., says Vespucci did invent a new astronomy based on the moon; so does Daniel Boorstin, *The Discoverers* (1983), ch. 33; Samuel Eliot Morison disagrees in *The European Discovery of America: The Southern Voyages* (1974), ch. 12.

7. Louis Simon, "Famous American Myths," *You're Wrong About That* (October 1938), p. 48, tells about "Amteric"; Thomas Jay, *The Encyclopedia of Fads and Fallacies* (1958), p. 12, tells about Ameryke.

8. Charles E. Nowell, "The Discovery of the Pacific: A Suggested Change of Approach," *Pacific Historical Review* (February 1947), pp. 1–10.

9. Bergen Evans, *The Spoor of Spooks* (1954), pp. 57–58.

10. Jerome E. Brooks, *The Mighty Leaf: Tobacco Through the Centuries* (1952), pp. 11, 46, 62–63.

11. Howard S. Abramson, *National Geographic: Behind America's Lens on the World* (1987), pp. 71–108.

12. Peter Baida, "Eli Whitney's Other Talent," *American Heritage* (May–June 1987), pp. 22–23.

13. Daniel H. Thomas, "Pre-Whitney Cotton Gins in French Louisiana," *Journal of Southern History* (May 1965), pp. 135–48; Thomas A. Bailey, "Presidential Address," *Journal of American History* (June 1968), p. 5ff.

14. Bernard Weisberger, communication with the author; Bureau of the Census, *A Century of Population Growth, from the First Census of the United States to the Twelfth, 1790–1900* (1909), pp. 133–40.

15. Alex Groner, *The American Heritage History of American Business and Industry* (1972), pp. 87–88; Ashley Montagu and Edward Darling, *The Prevalence of Nonsense* (1967), pp. 209–12.

16. Dixon Wecter, *The Hero in America* (1941), pp. 417–18.

17. *You're Wrong About That* (March 1939), p. 58.

18. Robert Lacey, *Ford: The Men and the Machine* (1986), pp. 110–17, 284; David Halberstam, *The Reckoning* (1986), passim; John Kenneth Galbraith, "Truly the Last Tycoons," *New York Review of Books* (August 14, 1986), p. 17.

19. Leonard Mosley, *Lindbergh* (1976), p. 73.

20. Peter Wyden, *Day One: Before Hiroshima and After* (1984), pp. 20–27.

Founding Fathers

1. Thomas A. Bailey, *The American Pageant* (1971), p. 195.

2. John Bach McMaster, "The Political Depravity of the Fathers," *Atlantic Monthly* (May 1895), pp. 626–33; Nathan Miller, *The Founding Finaglers* (1976), pp. 116–34.

3. Charles A. Beard, *The Republic* (1962), pp. 29–33.

4. Jack P. Greene, in an interview quoted in John A. Garraty, *Interpreting American History* (1970), vol. I, p. 55.

5. Henry Steele Commager, in an interview, ibid., vol. I, p. 103.

6. On Jefferson, see Charles B. Hosmer, *Presence of the Past* (1965), pp. 179–85; on Hamilton, Franklin, and Madison, see Michael Kammen, *A Season of Youth* (1978), pp. 42, 64, 69, 72; on Revere, see Dixon Wecter, *The Hero in America* (1941), p. 87; on Washington, see Daniel Boorstin, *The Americans: The National Experience* (1965), pp. 337–39, and W. E. Woodward, *George Washington* (1928), pp. 11, 239, 311.

Jefferson may have become a member of the national pantheon before the 1920's. At least Wecter thinks so. Wecter puts Jefferson's apotheosis in 1858, when a three-volume biography listing his major accomplishments was published. In any case, Jefferson seems unquestionably to have become a full-fledged member of the elite club of demigods (to use Jefferson's own term) by the 1930's. By then Gutzon Borglum had put his face on Mount Rushmore, the Jefferson Memorial had been built, and Jefferson's face had been put on the nickel in place of the buffalo. See Douglass Adair, *Fame and the Founding Fathers* (1974), pp. 239–40.

During the 1932 celebration of Washington's bicentennial, defenders of the first President took the opportunity to bash the debunkers who had been bashing Washington. Debunker Rupert Hughes came in for special vilification in the following poem:

> Let others echo Rupert Hughes
> And mix up motes and beams . . .
> The anecdotes that I peruse
> Were told by Parson Weems.
>
> Some minds affect the Freudian styles,
> Or Cherry-Orchard themes;
> The Cherry-Tree that still beguiles
> Is found in good old Weems.
>
> Above iconoclastic views
> That little hatchet gleams
> "I cannot tell a lie," I choose
> That Washington of Weems.

The poem can be found in the Bicentennial Commission's *Literature Series* (1932), vol. II, p. 545.

7. Rupert Hughes, *George Washington* (1930), vol. III, ch. 25; Adair, op. cit., pp. 145–49; Larzer Ziff, ed., *Benjamin Franklin's Autobiography* (1959), pp. x–xi. Hughes reports that Washington originally went to church but stopped going after the pastor criticized him for refusing to take communion, a religious practice with which Washington disagreed.

Presidents

1. The phrase "inveterate land-grabber" is Jonathan Clark's and can be found in "A Bicentennial Caution," *Vassar Quarterly* (Summer 1986), p. 76.

2. Richard B. Morris, *Seven Who Shaped Our Destiny* (1973), p. 50.

3. James Thomas Flexner, *George Washington* (1965), vol. I, p. 269; Hope Ridings Miller, *Scandals in the Highest Office* (1973), pp. 24–26, 49–54.

4. James Thomas Flexner, *George Washington and the New Nation* (1970), pp. 220–21; James Morton Smith, ed., *George Washington* (1969), p. 39.

5. Flexner, *George Washington*, vol. I, p. 193; vol II, pp. 499–500; vol. III, p. 204, vol. IV, pp. 308–17.

6. It may be worth pointing out that the story, silly as it is, is still taken seriously by Americans. Grown men, who wouldn't think of telling a story about Santa Claus at a public meeting, don't hesitate to mention the cherry tree story. There may be any number of reasons for this, but I suspect it's that Washington is considered so unassailable that even a fairy tale is deemed acceptable for a mature audience if he is the subject. When Senator Daniel K. Inouye referred to the cherry tree myth during the Iran-contra hearings in a

closing speech on the evil consequences of Lieutenant Colonel Oliver North's lies, not a single columnist took him to task. At least I couldn't find any after an extensive search through newspapers and magazines. The Inouye remark was made on July 14, 1987, on television.

7. Jefferson opposed the Sedition Act passed by Congress and signed by President John Adams on the ground that the federal government was restricted by the Constitution from limiting freedom of the press. But he believed the states weren't bound by the Bill of Rights and could do as they like. See Leonard Levy, *Jefferson and Civil Liberties* (1963), ch. 3.

8. Theodore Roosevelt is said to have been sorry Wilson, not he, revived the practice of addressing Congress in person. Clinton Rossiter, *The American Presidency* (1960), p. 99.

9. In 1796 an elector selected by the Federalists voted for Jefferson; in 1824 three New York electors pledged to Henry Clay voted against him. Arthur M. Schlesinger, *Paths to the Present* (1964), pp. 116, 120–21; Harvey Einbinder, *The Myth of the Britannica* (1964), pp. 174–75.

10. Richard Hofstadter, *The American Political Tradition* (1948), ch. 3.

11. John William Ward, *Andrew Jackson: Symbol for an Age* (1955), pp. 83–86.

12. Albert Somit, "Andrew Jackson: Legend and Reality," *Tennessee Historical Quarterly* (December 1948), pp. 291–313.

13. On the moon story, see Stephen B. Oates, *With Malice Toward None* (1977), pp. 141–42; on the looking-glass anecdote, see Lloyd Lewis, *Myths After Lincoln* (i.e., 1941), p. 293; on the beard, see Allan Nevins, *The Emergence of Lincoln: Prologue to Civil War, 1859–1861* (1950), p. 451.

14. Stephen B. Oates, *Abraham Lincoln: The Man Behind the Myths* (1984), p. 51.

15. Ibid., pp. 41–42; David Donald, *Lincoln Reconsidered* (1961), p. 156.

16. Dixon Wecter, *The Hero in America* (1941), p. 242; Stephen B. Oates, *With Malice Toward None* (1977), pp. 211–13; David Donald, *Lincoln's Herndon* (1948), p. 369n., on the *Sun* and *Tribune* stories.

17. Stefan Lorant, *Lincoln: A Picture Story of His Life* (1975), p. 200; Allan Nevins, *The War for the Union: The Organized War, 1863–1864* (1971), p. 448 n.

18. Donald, *Lincoln Reconsidered*, (p. 59); Lorant, op. cit., p. 199, cites the "foolish" quote.

19. Wecter, op. cit., pp. 249–51; Donald, *Lincoln Reconsidered*, pp. 144–66, includes a careful analysis of the folkloric Lincoln.

20. Thomas A. Bailey, *Probing America's Past* (1973), vol. II, p. 488. The quotation can be found in Charles S. Olcott, *The Life of William McKinley* (1916), vol. II, pp. 109–11.

21. David McCullough, *Mornings on Horseback* (1981), pp. 97, 101, 167; Hofstadter, op. cit., pp. 209–10.

22. Paul Johnson, *Modern Times* (1983), pp. 214–19; Frederick Lewis Allen, *Only Yesterday* (1931), ch. 6; Kenneth S. Lynn, "Only Yesterday," *American Scholar* (Autumn 1980), pp. 513–18; Eric F. Goldman, "A Sort of Rehabilitation of Warren G. Harding," *New York Times Magazine* (March 26, 1972), p. 42 ff.; Bailey, op. cit., vol. II, p. 191; Robert K. Murray, *The Politics of Normalcy* (1973), pp. 21–27, and *The Harding Era* (1969), pp. 36–41, 514–30; Francis Russell, "The Case That Will Not Close," *The New York Review of Books* (November 5, 1987), p. 10.

23. Alice Longworth denied making the pickle remark but said she agreed with it; see Bailey, op. cit., vol. II, p. 616 n. On other matters, see: Johnson, op. cit., p. 219; William

Shirer, *Twentieth Century Journey* (1976), pp. 224–25; Edward Latham, *Meet Calvin Coolidge* (1960), p. 158, on the Secret Service agent's recollection; Howard Quint and Robert Ferrell, eds., *The Talkative President* (1964), pp. 18, 19, on the press conference exchanges.

24. Bailey, op. cit., vol. II, pp. 634–39; Gene Smith, *The Shattered Dream* (1970), pp. 14–17. Reagan did *sound* like Hoover. *New York* magazine pointed out afterward that Reagan's comment that "the economic fundamentals in this country remain sound" echoed Hoover's line of fifty-seven years earlier: "The fundamental strength of the nation's economy is unimpaired." His advisers, however, vehemently denied Reagan was a Hoover type of President. "This guy is not Hoover," one was quoted as saying. "The first vote he ever cast was *against* Hoover. He's more like Roosevelt—in a crisis, he'll keep trying things until he finds something that works. I have no doubt that if he perceived a crisis, he would do what he had to do, even if it was in apparent opposition to everything he believes." Joe Klein, "Ronald Wilson Hoover?," *New York* (November 2, 1987), p. 41.

25. Fred Greenstein, "Debunking an Eisenhower Myth No One Believes," *Washington Post* Weekly Edition (September 22, 1986), p. 36; William Manchester, *American Caesar: Douglas MacArthur* (1978); Richard Nixon, *Six Crises* (1962), p. 161.

26. Blanche Wiesen Cook, "Clearly, Eisenhower Was a 'Militant Liberal,' " *The New York Times* (December 5, 1980), op-ed page.

27. Peter Collier and David Horowitz, *The Kennedys: An American Drama* (1984), pp. 175–76, 292–93.

28. Garry Wills, *The Kennedy Imprisonment* (1982), pp. 54, 129 ff.

29. William Leuchtenburg, "Ronald Reagan's Secret Liberal Past," *New Republic* (May 23, 1983), pp. 18–25; Garry Wills, *Reagan's America* (1987), p. 253 ff.

From Rags to Riches

1. Edward Pessen, *The Log Cabin Myth* (1984), passim; Garry Wills, *Reagan's America: Innocents at Home* (1987), pp. 55–63.

2. C. A. Weslager, *The Log Cabin in America* (1969), pp. 262, 274, 299–302, 307.

3. Herbert G. Gutman, "The Reality of the Rags-to-Riches Myth," in *Nineteenth-Century Cities*, ed. Stephan Thernstrom (1969), pp. 98–124.

4. Edward Pessen, ed., *The Many-Faceted Jacksonian Era* (1977), pp. 7–31.

5. David Hackett Fischer, *Historians' Fallacies* (1970), p. 172; Robert H. Bremner, *From the Depths* (1956), p. 126.

6. R. Richard Wohl, "The 'Country Boy' Myth and Its Place in American Urban Culture: The Nineteenth Century Contribution," *Perspectives in American History*, Charles Warren Center, Harvard (1969), vol. III, p. 126 ff.

Sex

1. Richard Lingeman, *Small Town America* (1980), p. 57.

2. The British variation on the theme was spelled out by Thomas Babington Macau-

lay, who remarked that the Puritans hated bearbaiting "not because it gave pain to the bear, but because it gave pleasure to the spectators."

3. Carl Degler, *Out of Our Past* (1970), pp. 9–20; Jerry Frost, lecture, Vassar College (Fall 1972); Gerald Carson, *The Polite Americans* (1966), p. 36.

4. It should be pointed out that bundling was done to save fuel used for heating; normally a board was placed between the pair to discourage sex.

5. Edmund S. Morgan, "Puritans and Sex," *New England Quarterly* (1942), pp. 591–607.

6. It may be worth noting that the Puritans approved of music and art as well as sex. According to Degler, op. cit., the Puritans introduced opera to England, approved of nude statuary, and even liked to dress well. As David Hackett Fischer observes in *Growing Old in America* (1978), pp. 35–36, business records indicate that only old Puritans wore black, drab clothes. Others wore clothes in bright colors, from "turkey red" to "royal purple." Fischer says Puritan women usually "decked themselves with red penistones, blue duffels, yellow flannels, and green aprons."

7. Richard Altick, *The Scholar Adventurers* (1950), pp. 244–48.

8. Carl Degler, *At Odds* (1980), pp. 249–78.

9. Roland Richard Wagner, "Virtue Against Vice" (Ph. D. dissertation, University of Wisconsin, 1971), pp. 16–17; Otto Bettman, *The Good Old Days—They Were Terrible* (1974), p. 98.

Sandy, Utah, is currently building a town museum in which the facts about its past will be candidly presented.

The guidebook can be found in the New-York Historical Society. It was printed privately and is dated 1870.

10. Wagner, op. cit., p. 216.

11. Page Smith, *The Rise of Industrial America* (1984), pp. 262–81.

12. Twain's speech, delivered in 1879, can be found in the New York Public Library. A note attached to the speech indicates it was suppressed until 1952, when it came into the hands of an advertising man who decided to have it printed. The speech is reprinted in its entirety in Richard Shenkman and Kurt Reiger, *One-Night Stands with American History* (1980), pp. 149–51.

13. Kenneth Lynn, "Only Yesterday," *American Scholar* (Autumn 1980), pp. 513–18; Frederick Lewis Allen, *Only Yesterday* (1931), ch. 5.

14. Lingeman, op. cit., pp. 268–69.

15. Degler, *At Odds*, ch. 10.

The Family

1. Information in this chapter, when not otherwise indicated, comes from Carl Degler, *At Odds* (1980), passim, especially pp. 66–85, 71–73, 144–77, and *Out of Our Past* (3d ed.; 1984), ch. 14, "The Shaping of American Families."

2. Edmund S. Morgan, *Puritan Family* (1944), passim. It should be pointed out that Puritans sent their male children away in order to be apprenticed.

3. David Hackett Fischer, *Growing Old in America* (1978), pp. 73–92. Fischer says

that hostility to the elderly was so pervasive that it even extended to the world of fashion. Before the Revolution "old age" was in fashion, and people liked to dress as if they were old even if they weren't. Coats emphasized sagging shoulders; pants were designed to demonstrate a wide girth. And as everyone knows, Americans liked to wear wigs, which gave a hint of venerable wisdom, whether or not one possessed any. After the elderly declined in esteem, fashion began to reflect youthful features. Pants were made tight at the hips, toupees began to be worn, and gray hair was dyed black.

Old people who committed the crime of looking old found themselves objects of curiosity—human antiques of a sort, though not in as much demand. There is the sorry case of Samuel Curwen, a Salem merchant, who suffered the misfortune of living past the Revolution after the elderly, so to speak, had gone out of style. "He appeared in our streets," one clergyman noted, "much like a Patriarch. The English tye-wig, the long scarlet cloak, the heavy rings, and gold-headed cane attracted notice after the war, tho' it was best dress before it, for persons of condition" (Fischer, op. cit., p. 88).

4. John Demos, *Past, Present, and Personal* (1986), p. 5, and A *Little Commonwealth: Family Life in Plymouth Colony* (1970), pp. 62–65, 74–76.

5. Frederick Lewis Allen, *The Big Change* (1952), p. 201.

6. Darrett B. and Anita H. Rutman, " 'Now-Wives and Sons-in-Law': Parental Death in a Seventeenth-Century Virginia County," in *The Chesapeake in the Seventeenth Century*, ed. Thad W. Tote and David L. Ammerman (1979), p. 153.

War

1. Dixon Wecter, *The Hero in America* (1941), p. 85.

2. Crane Brinton, *The Anatomy of Revolution* (1965), p. 176.

3. Wallace Brown, "The Loyalists and the American Revolution," in *Myth and the American Experience*, eds. Nicholas Cords and Patrick Gerster (2d ed., 1978), vol. I, p. 107.

4. Robert Gross, *The Minutemen and Their World* (1976), p. 150ff.

5. Wecter, op. cit., p. 82.

6. Stewart Holbrook, *Lost Men of American History* (1946), pp. 38–39.

7. Nathan Schachner, "Do School-Books Tell the Truth?" *American Mercury* (December 1938), pp. 416–17.

8. Don Higginbotham, "The Vietnamization of the American Revolution," *Historical Viewpoints: Notable Articles from American Heritage*, ed. John A. Garraty (1983), vol. I, pp. 168–71.

9. Wecter, op. cit., p. 97; Jonathan C. Clark, "A Bicentennial Caution," *Vassar Quarterly* (Summer 1986), p. 77.

10. Schachner, op. cit., pp. 415–16.

11. Wecter, op. cit., pp. 92, 498; Samuel Eliot Morison and Henry Steele Commager, *The Growth of the American Republic* (1937), pp. 136–37.

12. Schachner, op. cit., pp. 418–19.

13. Arthur Walworth, *School Histories at War* (1938), p. 246.

14. Ibid., ch. 2; John K. Mahon, *The War of 1812* (1972), p. 323.

15. Dan E. Kilgore, *How Did Davy Die?* (1978), passim; Walter Lord, *A Time to Stand* (1961), pp. 40, 60; William Zuber, *My Eighty Years in Texas* (1971), p. xi.

16. David Donald, *Lincoln Reconsidered* (1961), p. 82.

17. Frank Tannenbaum, *Slave and Citizen* (1946), p. 110; David Brion Davis, *The Problem of Slavery in Western Culture* (1966), p. 226.

18. Allan Nevins, *The War for the Union* (1971), vol. IV, p. 202; Roy Basler, ed., *Abraham Lincoln: His Speeches and Writings* (1946), pp. 766–77.

19. J. G. Randall and David Donald, *The Civil War and Reconstruction* (1961), pp. 336–37.

20. Robert McElroy, *Jefferson Davis: The Unreal and the Real* (1937), pp. 514–15.

21. Thomas A. Bailey, *Probing America's Past* (1973), vol. II, pp. 476–94, and *Essays Diplomatic and Undiplomatic* (1969), pp. 29–53.

22. Mark Sullivan, *Our Times* (1926), vol. I, pp. 309–38.

23. Arthur Hornblow, Jr., "The Amazing Armistice," *Century Magazine*, vol. CIII, (November 1921–April 1922), pp. 90–99.

24. Bailey, *Probing America's Past*, vol. II, pp. 530–77.

25. John Oliver, *History of American Technology* (1956), pp. 100–01; Roger Burlingame, *March of the Iron Men* (1938), pp. 146–48.

26. Bailey, *Probing America's Past*, vol. I, p. 405 n.; John Kenneth Galbraith, *A View from the Stands* (1986), pp. 318–19. The historian who wrote about the railroads and slavery is Robert Fogel; see David Hackett Fischer, *Historians' Fallacies* (1970), pp. 16–19.

27. Bailey, *Probing America's Past*, vol. II, pp. 574–77.

28. Ibid., vol. II, pp. 699–704.

29. A. J. P. Taylor, *A Personal History* (1984), p. 299; John Kenneth Galbraith, *A Life in Our Times* (1981), pp. 196–214. Galbraith: "The myth of ruthless Nazi competence established during the war years still endures. In reality, German war management was for a long time halfhearted and incompetent" (p. 204).

30. Taylor, op. cit., p. 299.

31. William J. Baker, *Jesse Owens* (1986), pp. 90–91.

32. David S. Wyman, *The Abandonment of the Jews* (1984), passim. "One does not wish to believe the facts," says Wyman. "America, the land of refuge, offered little succor. American Christians forgot about the Good Samaritan. Even American Jews lacked the unquenchable sense of urgency the crisis demanded. The Nazis were the murderers but we were all too passive accomplices" (p. xiii).

33. Paul Johnson, *Modern Times* (1983), p. 425; Galbraith, *Life*, pp. 232–33.

34. Peter Wyden, *Day One: Before Hiroshima and After* (1984), pp. 15–19.

35. Galbraith, *Life*, pp. 204–05.

36. Thomas A. Bailey, *The Man in the Street* (1948), p. 120.

37. There seems little point in trying to address the controversies about Vietnam that still divide liberals and conservatives, all of whom have their long lists of myths about the war. Thus I haven't tried to untangle the truth about such arcane issues as whether the Tet offensive of 1968 was a victory or defeat for America. This didn't seem the right place to do so. Those interested in the conservative viewpoint may consult Richard Nixon, *No More Vietnams* (1985), ch. 1. The liberal view is presented in Loren Baritz, *Backfire* (1985), passim.

38. Don Cook, *Charles de Gaulle* (1983), p. 349; Johnson, op. cit., p. 635. Barbara Tuchman makes the interesting point that the real tragedy of Vietnam is that we knew what

we were getting into and still plunged ahead anyway, heedless of the warnings of our friends and our own experts: "At no time were policy-makers unaware of the hazards, obstacles and negative developments. American intelligence was adequate, informed observation flowed steadily from the field to the capital, special investigative missions were repeatedly sent out, independent reportage to balance professional optimism—when that prevailed—was never lacking. The folly consisted not in pursuit of a goal in ignorance of the obstacles but in persistence in the pursuit despite accumulating evidence that the goal was unattainable, and the effect disproportionate to the American interest and eventually damaging to American society, reputation and disposable power in the world" (Barbara Tuchman, *The March of Folly* [1984], p. 234 ff.).

Immigrants

1. Daniel Patrick Moynihan, "What Wretched Refuse?," *New York* (May 12, 1986), p. 59.
2. Colin Greer, *The Greet School Legend* (1972), ch. 5. The statistics on Boston Jews are from Irving Howe, *World of Our Fathers* (1976), p. 141.
3. Richard Hofstadter and Michael Wallace, eds., *American Violence* (1971), pp. 304, 332; Thomas A. Bailey, *The American Pageant* (1971), pp. 577–80; Robert A. Caro, *The Power Broker: Robert Moses and the Fall of New York* (1974), p. 31, on the origin of the word "kike."
4. Howard Zinn, *A People's History of the United States* (1980), p. 373.
5. Bailey, op. cit., 582.
6. Not everyone agreed with Jay, notably Hector St. John de Crèvecoeur, the French immigrant farmer, who wrote about the "family whose grandfather was an Englishman, whose wife was Dutch, whose son married a French woman, and whose present four sons have now four wives of four different nations." Winthrop D. Jordan in *White over Black* (1968), pp. 336–39, says Crèvecoeur was in the minority; Jay, he says, represented the majority's opinion.
7. Ibid., Arthur Mann, "The Melting Pot," *Uprooted Americans: Essays to Honor Oscar Handlin*, ed. Richard L. Bushman et al. (1979), pp. 291–318; Nathan Glazer and Reed Ueda, *Ethnic Groups in History Textbooks* (1983), pp. 49–50; Paul Johnson, *Modern Times* (1983), p. 207.

The Frontier

1. Richard Lingeman, *Small Town America* (1980), p. 229; W. Eugene Hollon, *Frontier Violence: Another Look* (1974), pp. 194–216.
2. Ramon F. Adams, *More Burs Under the Saddle* (1979), pp. xii, 5, 21, 27, 55, 169; Dixon Wecter, *The Hero in America* (1941), ch. 13; Hollon, op. cit.
3. Wecter, op. cit., pp. 17–25; Alvin M. Josephy, ed., *The American Heritage Book*

of Indians (1982), p. 165; Alden Vaughan, "Beyond Pocahontas," *New York Times Book Review* (June 29, 1986), pp. 27–28.

4. Paul Sann, *Fads, Follies and Delusions of the American People* (1967), pp. 27–29; John Fischer, *The Stupidity Problem* (1964), pp. 219–22; Wecter, op. cit., pp. 189–93.

5. James Axtell and William C. Sturtevant, "The Unkindest Cut, or Who Invented Scalping?" *William and Mary Quarterly* (July 1980), pp. 451–72. Scalping, it should be noted, became accepted practice for Americans in the nineteenth century, if not earlier. Buffalo Bill in his road show used to feature the scalp he'd torn off the head of a young Indian chief whom he'd killed in a duel: "Jerking his war-bonnet off, I scientifically scalped him in about five seconds . . . and shouted, 'The first scalp for Custer!' " (quoted in Wecter, op. cit., p. 359).

6. Mark A. Mastromarino, "Teaching Old Dogs New Tricks: The English Mastiff and the Anglo-American Experience," *Historian* (November 1986), pp. 10–25.

7. Howard Zinn, *A People's History of the United States* (1980), p. 86.

8. James Axtell, "Colonial America Without the Indians: Counterfactual Reflections," *Journal of American History* (March 1987), pp. 981–96.

9. Carl Becker, *Every Man His Own Historian* (1966), p. 6.

10. William Bradford, *Of Plymouth Plantation*, ed. Harvey Wish (1962 ed.), p. 90; Alice Felt Tyler, *Freedom's Ferment* (1944), ch. 5.

11. James Truslow Adams, *The Epic of America* (1944), pp. 241–42.

12. Lingeman, op. cit., pp. 207–08.

13. Stuart Berg Flexner, *I Hear America Talking* (1976), pp. 276–77.

14. *Historical Statistics of the United States* (1960), p. 236.

From Slavery to Freedom

1. Ruth Scarborough, *The Opposition to Slavery in Georgia Prior to 1860* (1933; rpt. 1968), pp. 1–55.

2. David Brion Davis, *The Problem of Slavery in the Age of Revolution* (1975), pp. 23–32.

3. Jonathan C. Clark, "A Bicentennial Caution," *Vassar Quarterly* (Summer 1986), pp. 78–79; Davis, op. cit., pp. 24, 73, 76, 78–80.

4. Carl Degler, *The Other South* (1974), pp. 15–17.

5. John W. Blassingame, *The Slave Community* (1972), p. 2.

6. Kenneth M. Stampp, *The Peculiar Institution* (1956), pp. 104–05; Eugene D. Genovese, *Roll, Jordan, Roll* (1974), pp. 594–95. Stanley M. Elkins in *Slavery* (1959) argues that the slaves actually became sambos under slavery much in the same way that certain Jews in the concentration camps lost their individuality and identified with their captors. Elkins's work was imaginative; few think it was correct.

7. J. C. Furnas, *Goodbye to Uncle Tom* (1956), p. 20 ff.

8. Larry Gara, *The Liberty Line: The Legend of the Underground Railroad* (1961), passim.

9. Emory M. Thomas, *The Confederacy as a Revolutionary Experience* (1971), pp. 119–32.

10. Carl Degler, *Out of Our Past* (1962), pp. 219–27.

11. Genovese, op. cit., pp. 450–58.

12. Richard C. Wade, "America's Cities Are (Mostly) Better Than Ever," *American Heritage* (February–March, 1979), p. 10; Don Wycliff, "Going Under, Getting Ahead," *New York Times Book Review* (June 7, 1987), p. 12.

Education

1. Colin Greer, *The Great School Legend*, (1972), passim.

2. Barton Bledstein, *The Culture of Professionalism* (1976), p. 278.

3. Ibid., pp. 203–87.

4. Ibid., pp. 228–34.

5. Harvey Einbinder, *The Myth of the Britannica* (1964), passim.

Holidays

1. Catherine Drinker Bowen, *John Adams* (1950), p. 598 n.; Marshall Smelser, "The Glorious Fourth—or, Glorious Second? or Eighth?," *Myth and the American Experience*, eds. Nicholas Cords and Patrick Gerster (1978), vol. I, pp. 101–6; Charles Warren, "Fourth of July Myths," *William and Mary Quarterly* (July 1945), pp. 242–48.

2. Allan Nevins, *The Gateway to History* (1962), pp. 137–38.

3. The only direct testimony available about the first Thanksgiving is contained in a letter Edward Winslow wrote to a friend in England on December 11, 1621. The part of the letter concerning Thanksgiving reads in its entirety as follows: "Our harvest being gotten in, our Governor sent four men on fowling, that so we might after a more special manner rejoice together, after we had gathered the fruit of our labours. They four in one day killed as much fowl as, with a little help beside, served the Company almost a week. At which time, amongst other recreations, we exercised our arms, many of the Indians coming amongst us, and amongst the rest their greatest king, Massasoit with some 90 men, whom for three days we entertained and feasted. And they went out and killed five deer which they brought to the plantation and bestowed on our Governor and upon the Captain and others." The letter is quoted in William Bradford, *Of Plymouth Plantation: 1620–1647*, ed. Samuel Eliot Morison (1952), p. 90 n. See also William DeLoss Love, Jr., *The Fast and Thanksgiving Days of New England* (1895), pp. 70–75; Robert J. Myers, *Celebrations: The Complete Book of American Holidays* (1972), p. 276; and Roland G. Usher, *The Pilgrims and Their History* (1920), p. 93.

4. Daniel J. Boorstin, *The Americans: The Democratic Experience* (1973), p. 158.

Shrines

1. Charles Warren, "Fourth of July Myths," *William and Mary Quarterly* (July 1945), pp. 248–54; Daniel Boorstin, *The Americans: The National Experience* (1965), pp. 381–82; *American Heritage* (June 1973), p. 104; Victor Rosewater, *The Liberty Bell* (1926), passim.
2. Richard Ketchum, ed., *The American Heritage History of the American Revolution* (1971), pp. 106–09.
3. Arthur Lord, *Plymouth and the Pilgrims* (1920), pp. 120–21; Samuel Eliot Morison, *By Land and by Sea* (1953), p. 307.
4. Charles B. Hosmer, Jr., *Presence of the Past* (1965), pp. 140–45; C. A. Weslager, *The Log Cabin in America* (1969), pp. 289–91.
5. Hosmer, op. cit., pp. 88–92; Harvey Einbinder, *The Myth of the Britannica* (1964), pp. 359–61.
6. Einbinder, op. cit., p. 361.
7. Michael Wallace, "Visiting the Past," *Preserving the Past: Essays on History and the Public,* ed. Susan Porter Benson et al. (1986), pp. 137–39.
8. Ibid., pp. 142–47.

Art

1. Charles Henry Hart, "Frauds in Historical Portraiture," *Annual Report,* American Historical Association (1913), vol. I, pp. 85–99; Henry C. Shelley, *John Harvard and His Times* (1907), pp. 312–13; on Appleseed, see Dixon Wecter, *The Hero in America* (1941), p. 195.
2. Wecter, op. cit., p. 187.
3. Robert M. Utley and Wilcomb E. Washburn, *The American Heritage History of the Indian Wars* (1977), p. 12; W. A. Graham, *The Custer Myth* (1953), p. xiii.
4. Even normally skeptical Americans like Nathaniel Hawthorne fell in with the mythologizing crowd when it came to Washington. When he came across one of the portraits in England, Hawthorne remarked that he was "proud to see that noblest face and figure here in England; any English nobleman would look like common beef or clay beside him." See Marshall W. Fishwick, *American Heroes: Myth and Reality* (1954), ch. 4; Wecter, op. cit., p. 114; Rudolph Marx, *The Health of the Presidents* (1960), pp. 17–18; Daniel Boorstin, *The Americans: The National Experience* (1965), pp. 337–56; George Washington Parke Custis, "Portraits of Washington," in *Recollections and Private Memoirs of Washington* (1860), pp. 516–31; James Thomas Flexner, *George Washington* (1972), vol. IV, p. 310; Alfred W. McCann, *Greatest of Men: Washington* (1927), pp. 173–74. The biographer who commissioned the new portrait of Washington was William Wilbur, *The Making of George Washington* (1970).

5. Robert Caro, *The Power Broker: Robert Moses and the Fall of New York* (1974), in a note accompanying the photo.

6. Stefan Lorant, *Lincoln: A Picture Story of His Life* (1975), pp. 306–07.

7. Hiller B. Zobel, *The Boston Massacre* (1970), pp. 198–99. I am indebted to Harry Ahearn for pointing out the significance of the little dog.

8. Stewart Holbrook, *Lost Men of American History* (1946), pp. 35–36.

9. Weems's account tells how Potts, supposedly an eyewitness, caught Washington praying: "Treading his way along the venerable grove, suddenly he heard the sound of a human voice, which, as he advanced, increased on his ear; and at length became like the voice of one speaking much in earnest. As he approached the spot with a cautious step, whom should he behold, in a dark natural bower of ancient oaks, but the commander in chief of the American armies on his knees at prayer! Motionless with surprise, friend Potts continued on the place til the general, having ended his devotions, arose; and with a countenance of angelic serenity, retired to headquarters. Friend Potts then went home, and on entering his parlour called out to his wife, 'Sarah! my dear Sarah! all's well! all's well! George Washington will yet prevail!' " See Rupert Hughes, *George Washington* (1930), vol. III, ch. 25; Hughes devotes the entire chapter to refuting the Weems story.

10. Barbara S. Groseclose, *Emanuel Leutze, 1816–1868: Freedom Is the Only King* (1975), p. 33 ff., says it doesn't matter if the painting isn't completely accurate; what counts is that Americans love it. The painting is probably worth more to the average museum visitor, she says, "than six alleys full of masterpieces such as 'Boy in a Blue Hat Rolling a Hoop,' 'Young Girl Peeling an Apple' or even Rembrandt's 'Old Woman Cutting Her Nails.' Anyone who would pan the painting would denounce the Lincoln Memorial on the ground that one of the hairs in Lincoln's head was not there on August 10, 1862, at half past three!"

Not everyone has agreed, of course. Not even the Metropolitan Museum of Art, which owns the original. In the early 1930's the museum stowed the painting in the basement for several years to make room for other works. William Sloane Coffin, the museum president, said in his opinion "Washington Crossing the Delaware" was "neither history nor art."

11. Ann Hawkes Hutton, *Portrait of Patriotism* (1959), pp. 45, 85, 107, 112, 144 ff.

12. Lucius Beebe, "Pandemonium at Promontory," *American Heritage* (February 1958), p. 20 ff.

13. Wecter, op. cit., pp. 35–36. Wecter says the truth about the log cabin was discovered by Robert R. Shurtleff, the former head of the research department at Williamsburg, as long ago as 1939. The information, however, has yet to seep into the American mind. A major New York department store featured in one of its Christmas windows a classic Pilgrim family dinner—in a log cabin.

The Good Old Days

1. Charles Silberman, "What You Didn't Know About Criminal Justice," *American Heritage* (June 1982), p. 84; Otto Bettmann, *The Good Old Days—They Were Terrible* (1974), pp. 87–108. Bergen Evans, *The Spoor of Spooks* (1954), pp. 201–02.

2. David J. Rothman, "Poverty in America," *Historical Viewpoints*, ed. John Garraty (1983), vol. I, p. 305.

3. Bettmann, op. cit., p. 43.

4. Frederick Lewis Allen, *The Big Change* (1952), p. 144; Ruth Schwartz Cowan, *More Work for Mother* (1983), pp. 181, 194–95. Poverty in the Reagan years reportedly increased, but the rate is still nowhere near the level recorded even twenty-five years ago.

5. I am quoting Cowan, op. cit., pp. 195–96.

6. It's estimated that in 1876, the year of the centennial, 12 to 14 percent of the working people who wanted jobs couldn't find one; in 1894, 18 percent of the work force was unemployed. See Burton J. Bledstein, *The Culture of Professionalism* (1976), p. 46; Edward Chase Kirkland, *Dream and Thought in the Business Community* (1956), p. 9; David Donald, "Our Irrelevant History," *The New York Times* (September 8, 1977), op-ed page.

7. Bettmann, op. cit., pp. 1–18.

8. David Hackett Fischer, *Historians' Fallacies* (1970), pp. 170–71; Douglas E. Leach, *Flintlock and Tomahawk* (1966), pp. 243–44.

9. Bettmann, op. cit., pp. 152–53.

Folklore

1. I am quoting Dixon Wecter, *The Hero in America* (1941), p. 348. Casey's story is briefly told in Richard Dorson, *American Folklore* (1977), pp. 231–32.

2. Robert Cromie, *The Great Chicago Fire* (1958), pp. 24–34.

3. Dorson, op. cit., pp. 232–36; Wecter, op. cit., pp. 193–98.

4. Charles Panati, *Extraordinary Origins of Everyday Things* (1987), pp. 274–77.

5. Iona Opie and Peter Opie, eds., *The Oxford Dictionary of Nursery Rhymes* (1952), pp. 37–42.

6. Daniel Hoffman, *Paul Bunyan: Last of the Frontier Demigods* (1952), points out that Laughead's stories became popular only when he turned Bunyan into a kind of twentieth-century industrial capitalist; two early stories in which Bunyan was more lumberjack than accountant failed to achieve popular success. See also Richard Dorson, *American Folklore and the Historian* (1971), pp. 8–9, and *American Folklore*, pp. 216–26.

7. Panati, op. cit., pp. 72–75; Albert Bigelow Paine, *Th. Nast: His Period and His Pictures* (1904), p. 22.

Famous Quotes

1. Arthur M. Schlesinger, *Nothing Stands Still* (1969), pp. 94–97.

2. Douglass Adair, *Fame and the Founding Fathers* (1974), p. 244.

3. Tom Burnam, *The Dictionary of Misinformation* (1975), p. 116.

4. Nathan Schachner, "Do School-Books Tell the Truth?" *American Mercury* (De-

cember 1938), pp. 415–16; Willis Thornton, *Fable, Fact and History* (1957), pp. 122–23.

5. William Ander Smith, "Henry Adams, Alexander Hamilton, and the American People as a 'Great Beast,' " *New England Quarterly* (June 1975).

6. Thomas A. Bailey, *Voices of America* (1976), p. 36; Henry F. Woods, *American Sayings* (1949), pp. 12–13.

7. Allan Nevins, *The Gateway to History* (1962), p. 150.

8. Paul F. Boller, *Quotemanship* (1967), p. 331.

9. Ibid.

10. Clifford May, "Biden and the Annals of Raised Eyebrows," *New York Times* (September 21, 1987), p. 12; Burnam, op. cit., p. 110.

11. David Homer Bates, *Lincoln Stories* (1926), pp. 49–50; Burnam, op. cit., pp. 110–11.

12. Henry Luther Stoddard, *Horace Greeley*, p. 40; Glyndon G. Van Deusen, *Horace Greeley* (1953), p. 173; William Harlan Hale, *Horace Greeley* (1950), pp. 195–96; *Bartlett's* (1948), p. 505; Bergen Evans, *Dictionary of Quotations* (1968), p. 745; Joseph Conlin, *Morrow Book of Quotations in American History* (1984), p. 128.

13. James A. Barnes, "Myths of the Byran Campaign," *Mississippi Valley Historical Review* (1947), passim.

14. Thornton, op. cit., pp. 119–20.

15. Ibid., pp. 117–18.

16. Morris Kominsky, *The Hoaxers* (1970), pp. 27–34.

17. Ibid., p. 40.

18. Conrad Teitell, "Was Biden an Echo?," *The New York Times* (September 1987), op-ed page.

19. Boller, op. cit., p. 344.

20. Ibid., p. 353.

Index

British, 64, 80, 84, 86, 88–89, 99, 110–11, 114, 117, 118, 121, 127, 139, 140, 145, 154, 155, 173
Britton, Nan, 49
Brookings Institution, 160
Brown, A. W., 27
Brown, John, 47
Bryan, William Jennings, 176–77
Buchanan, James, 61
Buffalo Bill, 113
Bunker Hill, Battle of, 144–45
Burr, Aaron, 36

Cabot, John, 15, 17
Calhoun, John C., 154
Cano, Juan Sebastián del, 18
Cantwell, Robert, 179
Capone, Al, 73
Carnegie, Andrew, 63
Carter, Jimmy, 62
Casey Jones, 165
Castrillón, General Manuel Fernández, 90
Catherine the Great, 87
Cattell, James, 130
Causici, Enrico, 151
Central Pacific Railroad, 156
Chapman, John, 151, 166
Chinese, 18, 83, 110, 179
Christmas, 141–42, 168–69
Cinderella, 167
Civil War, 23, 64, 71, 91–93, 95–96, 125, 141, 148, 169
Clay, Henry, 154
Clemens, Samuel, 70, 73, 128
Clermont, 24
Cleveland, Grover, 59, 61, 62, 73
Clinton, George, 31
Cody, Bill, 113
Columbus, Christopher, 13–17, 19, 150
Communism, 106, 118, 178
Comstock, Anthony, 69, 72, 73
Confederacy, 93, 95–96, 125–27
Confederate Congress, 127
Constitution, U.S., 30, 172
Constitutional Convention, 24, 33
Continental Congress, 36, 122, 138, 172
Cook, Frederick, 19–21
Cook, Captain James, 151
Coolidge, Calvin, 52–53, 62, 153
Cooper, Kent, 74
Cotton, John, 68
Cotton gin, 22–23

Crédit Mobilier, 30, 128
Crime, 158–60
Crockett, Davy, 89–90, 114
Cuba, 110
Custer, George, 151–52

Daugherty, Harry, 50
Daughters of the American Revolution, 34, 83
Davenport, John, 146
Davids, Jules, 56
Davis, Jefferson, 92, 93, 127, 146
Dawes, William, 87
Deane, Silas, 87
Debs, Eugene V., 50
Declaration of Independence, 33–34, 59, 139–40, 148, 151, 170
De Gaulle, Charles, 106
Degler, Carl, 69, 75, 77–80, 123
Demos, John, 79
Dennett, Alfred W., 146
Dewey, George, 94
De Witt, Richard Varick, 24
Discoveries: America, 13–17; Hudson River, 18–19; North Pole, 19–21; Pacific Ocean, 18; tobacco, 19
Divorce, 80–82
Donald, David, 91, 162
Doolittle and Earle, 155
Dorson, Richard, 166, 168
Douglas, Stephen, 174
Drake, Francis Samuel, 34
Dreiser, Theodore, 74
Drugs, 163–64
Dunmore, Lord, 121–22
Dutch, 97, 168–69

Edison, Thomas, 24, 149
Eisenhower, Dwight D., 54–55, 62
Eliot, Charles William, 135
Emancipation Proclamation, 46, 121, 126
Emerson, Ralph Waldo, 17, 84–85
Encyclopædia Britannica, 13, 126, 136
Ericsson, Leif, 15, 17
Erie Railroad Company, 24

Fairfax, Sally, 38
Faunce, Thomas, 145
FBI, 57
Federalists, 30, 34, 36, 41, 110–11
Fellows, Henry, 31
Fillmore, Millard, 61